Be Different!

Be Different!

The Key to Business and Career Success

Stan Silverman

BEP BUSINESS EXPERT PRESS

Be Different! The Key to Business and Career Success

Copyright © Business Expert Press, LLC, 2019.

Cover Image Credit: JuSun/iStock/Getty Images

First published in 2019 by
Business Expert Press, LLC
222 East 46th Street, New York, NY 10017
www.businessexpertpress.com

ISBN-13: 978-1-94999-174-1 (paperback)
ISBN-13: 978-1-94999-175-8 (e-book)

Business Expert Press Business Career Development Collection

Collection ISSN: 2642-2123 (print)
Collection ISSN: 2642-2131 (electronic)

Cover and interior design by Exeter Premedia Services Private Ltd., Chennai, India

First edition: 2019

10 9 8 7 6 5 4 3 2 1

Printed in the United States of America.

Endorsements

Stan Silverman's advice in *Be Different! The Key to Business and Career Success* will not only lead to business and career success as the title suggests, but will lead to a more purposeful and fulfilling life. I've known Stan for nearly two decades. During that time his company was a key supplier to our company, and we worked together on industry association boards.

Stan is one of the most value-centered, outstanding leaders I know. I've seen him live the messages of his book first-hand. This excellent book has great advice. Marching to a different drummer, being values-centered, doing the "harder right rather than the easier wrong" will not only differentiate you as a leader but lead to differentiated results and happiness. Study and put to practice this book.

Robert A. McDonald
8th Secretary of the Department of Veteran Affairs
Retired Chairman, President, and CEO of
The Procter & Gamble Company

Over the course of three decades as Publisher of *Directors & Boards*, I have had the opportunity to review many business books, but few have been as informative and instructive as Stan Silverman's recent publication, *Be Different!*. Having served on Stan's board when he was President and CEO of PQ Corporation, a large, highly successful global chemical company, I had eagerly awaited the publication of his book which provides valuable lessons on how to be an effective leader. My expectations were exceeded!

For the past several years, I have read his nationally syndicated column, which dispenses valuable and practical guidance for top executives. Stan's advice is spot on, as only someone who "has been there" can deliver. *Be Different!* is a must-read for corporate leaders who are trying to differentiate their companies and themselves. Learn from Stan's wealth of experience to advance both your business and your career.

Robert H. Rock
Chairman
MLR Media
Publisher, *Directors & Boards*

Be Different! adds incredible value in an environment devoid of doing things right for the right reason. It provides guidance on how to cut through the bureaucracy and red tape that stifle transformative change and sets the bar for individual and organizational excellence. Finally, we now have a compilation of the astute wisdom of a seasoned C-Suite executive whose life-long work has been focused on driving results by developing leaders through his professional experience, innate intuitiveness, clear communication and heartfelt EQ.

Stan's advice never grows old. I have personally learned and benefited through real life interaction and observation. My files contain many of his columns cut and pasted for quick reference. They have rescued me many times! His writings contain first-hand advice and direction worth more than any MBA. This is a must-read handbook for any aspiring leader as well as current executives.

Judith Spires

CEO

KB US Holdings

If you are looking for a book about leadership, one that combines knowledge and experience, you will want to read *Be Different!* by Stan Silverman. Stan knows about leadership from all angles—from bottom up and top down, from process engineer to chief executive officer, and from inside out and outside in, as board member and columnist.

His leadership lessons—the importance of setting the tone at the top, building a culture of trust, and empowering people, to name a few—are invaluable for us all, no matter where we stand in the organizational hierarchy.

Anne M. Greenhalgh, Ph.D.

Deputy Director, McNulty Leadership Program, The

Wharton School, University of Pennsylvania

Co-Host, Leadership in Action, SXM Radio

It is a rare person that becomes a CEO. Even achieving that leadership position is not an assurance of success. The landscape is littered with CEO's that didn't achieve the greatness the board anticipated. One can imagine how often goals allude even successful CEO's.

Stan is the rare individual who became successful as a CEO. Even rarer, he is able to mentor other executives with timely insights through his writing. Most business writers observed good leaders and wrote about them. Stan was a great CEO who is also a uniquely good writer who can pass along his insights effectively.

Brian R. Ford
Retired EY partner
Independent Board Member

If you want to be successful in business, career or life, be different. Be different in how you lead, how you negotiate, how you listen. Emerson said, "Do not go where the path may lead, go where there is no path and leave a trail." Stan Silverman tells you how. Buy the book and devour it, internalizing then executing on the best advice you are likely to ever receive.

Dianne L. Semingson
Founder and CEO
DLS International

In today's fast-paced, ultra-competitive business environment, leadership at the top is a key, sustainable differentiator. Stan's book helps the leaders of today and tomorrow understand the values, passion and persistence required to make a real difference to help your company become the preferred provider of products or services to the market.

Mike Lawrie,
CEO
DXC Technology

"Speaking truth to power" has taken on a new meaning in our current business, political and cultural environment. *Be Different!* urges all leaders to set the right tone at the top, nurture the right organizational culture and respect and listen to those within their organizations who speak their mind and share their views, even if contrary to the views of the leader. Leaders who ignore these lone wolfs do so at their own peril and that of the organization.

Stan Silverman teaches this and other valuable lessons to business leaders for creating competitive advantage, and shows individuals how to differentiate themselves from their peers to win that next job and advance in their careers.

Stephen S. Tang
President and Chief Executive Officer
OraSure Technologies, Inc.

Stan Silverman has produced an unconventional tour de force in his book, *Be Different!*. The book is unique: it is neither a get-rich-quick manual nor is it an erudite rendition of strategic concepts, but is rather a set of integrated principles to build one's career with honor and integrity.

In addition to analyzing some well-publicized examples of business mistakes, e.g., Starbucks, Theranos and Turing Pharmaceuticals, Silverman weaves in lessons from his own very successful career, starting as a junior engineer and becoming the CEO of a major global corporation.

At a time when shareholder value is touted as the only goal of a business, Silverman brings the focus back to the need for values and for adhering to the golden rule on the road to success. His discussion of nurturing culture and the need to eject tyrants is a must read for aspiring leaders.

For students planning their careers, Silverman's advice on being different is timely. This book should find a prominent place on the desks of placement officers and career counselors in schools and colleges.

V.K. Narayanan
Deloitte Touche Jones Stubbs Professor of Strategy and Entrepreneurship
LeBow College of Business
Drexel University

Stan Silverman's *Be Different!* is chock-full of life lessons on personal development, building sustainable businesses, and what it means to be a leader. In today's world of "shock and awe," Stan thoughtfully reminds us of the importance of how we treat the people in our lives if we want to succeed in life and business.

Mike Williams
Chairman
Realogy Holdings Corporation

In Stan Silverman's *Be Different! The Key to Business and Career Success*, you have a very detailed and comprehensive guide to follow in your journey throughout your career. The author shares his personal experiences from curious child to successful CEO of a major international enterprise and captures the essence of the fundamental qualities necessary in being a successful student, employee, co-worker, manager and leader.

These lessons learned through experience, and not in a textbook or a classroom, are very valuable and applicable to all career paths not solely in private, for-profit organizations. This compendium, with subtlety, recognizes that capability is the key to success. That capability is comprised of ability, which can be acquired, and skill, which is a combination of natural talent, such as intuitive and experience-based judgement. It encourages you to manage, control and follow your intuition. Follow this well written, in-depth treatise and you will achieve your dream.

Chuck Pennoni, PE
Chairman of the Board
Pennoni Associates

Be Different! is concisely written, to the point and an easy read for the busy professional. Stan Silverman demonstrates that the key trait in highly successful leaders is emotional intelligence. His book gives you the insights that you need to set the right leadership tone from the top while creating an overall culture and driving success with your team. Stan encourages you to achieve success by being different.

Having been an avid fan of Stan's columns in the *Philadelphia Business Journal*, I couldn't wait to read his book. Share this book with your colleagues and local leaders and organizations that recognize that the rapidly changing business environment requires us all to build a better competitive edge so that our businesses and economy can thrive.

Emily Bittenbender
Managing Partner
Bittenbender Construction, LP

Be Different! focuses on business traits and leadership skills that helps businesses as well as current and aspiring leaders differentiate themselves in a competitive and ever-changing marketplace. As the CEO of an engineering firm, I appreciate Silverman's focus on ethics and integrity, often overlooked but essential to sustained business and personal success. *Be Different!* provides practical guidance and advice, supported by Silverman's real-life experiences, as a young professional, CEO and board member.

Kenneth R. Fulmer
President and CEO
Urban Engineers

Be Different! is a compelling description of the characteristics and strategies necessary for a CEO's in today's competitive environment. From cover to cover Stan provides a roadmap for navigating the challenges of successful organizations. If you want to continue to evolve as a leader, then this book is your reference guide.

Charles Pizzi
Former President and CEO, Tasty Baking Company
Independent Board Member

This book is dedicated to my grandchildren Andrew, Lauren, Aidan, and Sydney Ruth. I hope they live their lives making a difference in the lives of others to make this world a better place, as I have tried to do. There is no higher calling.

Abstract

The fundamental goal of any business is to be different—to be better than those with whom it is competing. Every company should be on a journey to be the preferred provider of products or services to its markets by offering a great customer/client experience. A preferred provider is the company that customers and clients preferentially want to do business with, and often can charge a premium for what they provide.

The fundamental goal of any individual is to be different—to be better than those with whom they are competing for that next job, whether internally or externally at a new company. Their goal is to demonstrate to the hiring manager that they are the best choice for that position.

This book teaches leaders of companies how to be different than their competitors and individuals pursuing their careers how to be different than their peers, based on personal experience serving in the trenches as a CEO as well as a board member of successful global corporations.

Keywords

leadership; leader; manager; ceo; coo; director; tone; tone at the top; trust; culture; ethics; integrity; continuous improvement; emotional intelligence; comfort zone; lone wolf; ownership; tyrant; preferred provider; customer experience; personal brand; network; attitude; career success; whistle blower; hotline; entrepreneurship; toxic boss; toxic organization; tone deaf; customer service

Contents

Acknowledgments

Writing a book requires dedicated support from many people. I would like to thank all those individuals who have played a part in what is my third and current career as a nationally syndicated columnist. I want to thank American City Business Journals and *Philadelphia Business Journal* for permission to use the content of my articles in this book.

I am certainly a product of my professional career and the opportunities afforded to me. Many thanks to the Evans and Elkinton families, the former owners of PQ Corporation, a global producer of commodity chemicals, specialty chemicals, catalysts, and engineered glass materials, for placing their trust and having faith in me as I rose up through the organization to the position of chief executive officer. The value system of PQ stemmed from the founder's Quaker beliefs to "dwell under the proper regard for the best things." These values have had a lasting impact on my personal value system.

Tim Elkinton and Morrie Evans, the patriarchs of each family, were early mentors to me. Many thanks to their sons, Buzz Elkinton and Joe Evans, my contemporaries and friends, who assumed the roles of their fathers after they retired. I also thank the directors who served on the board of PQ during my tenure as chief operating officer and chief executive officer for their wisdom and guidance.

PQ was a great company at which to work. I learned much from the leaders to whom I reported as well as from my direct reports. At times, I was subjected to tough love, which was uncomfortable at the time, but in retrospect, I needed. I thank the many colleagues I had the pleasure to interface with. We grew and developed our careers together.

Many thanks to Donna De Carolis, founding dean of Drexel University's Charles D. Close School of Entrepreneurship, the first stand-alone degree granting school of entrepreneurship in the United States. Donna invited me on the Close School's inaugural trip to Silicon Valley in March 2014, with 6 staff members and 16 of her students. We visited Apple, eBay, PayPal and we met many entrepreneurs at incubators, accelerators, and co-working spaces. The Close School's students inspired me to get out of my comfort zone and take on a new challenge as a writer about my business experiences. I thank them for changing my paradigms to do something new.

I am indebted to former *Philadelphia Business Journal* editor-in-chief Craig Ey and former publisher Lyn Kremer for giving me an opportunity and the platform to write for the digital edition of their newspaper. I also want to thank Sandy Smith, the current publisher of *Philadelphia Business Journal,* for his advice and guidance, as well as former managing editors Jared Shelly, Dell Poncet, and Kevin Donahue.

Many thanks to Craig for recommending me for national syndication in the 43 American City Business Journals across the United States. I am grateful to Craig and the national syndication editors that I have had— Ed Stych, David Arnott, Jeff Jeffery, Mark Mensheha, and Ben Eubanks for their advice and guidance to this columnist who has never had any formal journalism training.

I thank my two editors, Julia Casciato, former editor-in-chief of *The Triangle*, Drexel University's independent student newspaper, and Alexa Josaphouitch, former co-chief copy editor of *The Triangle*, who edit my column each week and edited this book. I appreciate their advice and guidance to me, who, at the beginning, was this neophyte writer.

I would like to thank Leo Levinson who oversaw public relations as I started this journey and for helping conceive Silverman Leadership, the vehicle I use for speaking engagements and coaching leaders. I also want to thank Karin Copeland, founder and CEO of Create X Change, who has given me invaluable advice and guidance as I develop my career as a published author. Many thanks to Elisa Frischling, former CEO of Lipo Chemicals, one of my former clients, for encouraging me to write this book.

I appreciate and thank my son Rob and wife Jackie for taking the last look at my columns before I submit them for weekly publication. Jackie, thank you for putting up with me during my professional career, and for your support and encouragement to write this book.

Argyle Interactive is the digital media company that manages my website and sends out over 1,200 e-mails with my column each week. I thank Argyle co-founder Dean Mahmoud and co-founder and CEO

Logan Levenson for their advice and guidance. I also thank Jon Shettsline, Argyle's e-mail and analytics manager, for his expertise, creativity, and advice to increase my readership.

Many thanks to my literary editor Vilma Barr for her advice, guidance, and tireless work reviewing multiple drafts of this book to ensure I communicate my experiences to my readers in the best possible way.

Last of all, I want to thank my readers who comment after each article and share their views. They may not agree with what I write, but the interchange we have helps us both understand a different point of view. We need more of this type of dialogue in this world.

Stan Silverman
November 2, 2019

My Journey

What compels anyone to write a book? It takes a significant amount of time and focus, and if the subject matter of the book is autobiographical in nature, it takes a willingness to share with readers personal things about yourself that are private and have never been shared in public.

I am fortunate to have experienced four careers: first, rising up through PQ Corporation and eventually becoming its chief executive officer; second, as a board member of public, private, private equity, trade association, and nonprofit boards; third, currently as a columnist on leadership, and corporate governance, and fourth, as an author of this book that will help others be successful by sharing my observations and experiences. I have learned many lessons along the way about people, life, and myself.

Early Years

I grew up in the northeast section of Philadelphia, the first born of Sidney and Ruth Silverman. We were middle class, as were my parents' friends. Few were college graduates. Thinking back to my childhood years, there were few professional role models who were friends of the family. However, they were role models in other ways. They stressed the importance of education, hard work, honesty, ethics, and integrity, and these traits formed the basis of my value system. It is one of the reasons why I am a strong advocate of ethics and integrity in the workplace.

My dad was an entrepreneur, even though we never referred to him as one. He ran a small electrical supply business, providing lighting and electrical products to industrial and commercial customers. On many occasions, I would accompany my dad visiting his customers, watching him differentiate his business through a high level of customer service.

When I think back over this period of my life and about what influenced my development, I believe it was the independence that was granted to me and the freedom to explore, to try things that interested me, and to learn from mistakes. Unlike today, where so many kids have helicopter parents managing their organized activities, kids growing up in the late 1950s and early 1960s had the freedom and independence to explore with their friends all types of unorganized activities and interests. We played baseball and touch football at Solly Avenue playground about a mile from where I lived. We all rode our bikes there. No adults were involved. We figured it out as we played.

My younger brother Stuart and I used the odds and ends of lumber stored in our garage to build the frame of a go-cart and attached the wheels of an old baby stroller. Stuart and I raced our friends down steeply sloped Mower Street, a block from our house on Tustin Avenue. There were no parents involved to help us build these vehicles. We used our own creativity, and when we found we didn't have the fastest go-cart, we figured out why, made modifications, and hoped that races the next day would yield a better result.

With the exception of spending a week at Treasure Island Boy Scout Camp during the ages of 11 and 12, and seven weeks at Sun Mountain overnight camp at the age of 13, I spent much of my summers hanging out with friends, riding our bikes, and exploring the neighborhoods near where we lived. This was a time of no iPhones or Androids. I would leave the house at 9 a.m. and was told by my mom to be back home prior to dinner. No one kept track of where my friends and I were during the day. At lunch time, we would show up to have lunch at one of our homes. This experience exploring surrounding neighborhoods was invaluable in building independence.

My dad was very supportive of me as I pursued my interest in science. When I was 13, he purchased a Gilbert chemistry set for me, which taught basic experiments in chemistry. After exhausting all of the experiments in the book, I wanted to do something more interesting.

After deciding where my curiosity would next take me, I asked my dad to purchase the chemicals needed to make gun powder, the key ingredient of a firecracker. I decided I would formulate the powder and pack it into a small cardboard cylindrical tube about 1.5 inches long and an inch in diameter which lined the inside of a device called a starter that turned on fluorescent lighting fixtures. Since my dad was in the electrical supply business, I had an endless supply of these small cylindrical tubes.

Being very leery about setting off the powder in the tubes at close range, this future chemical engineering student designed his own remote fuse. I used the 18-volt current from my Lionel model train transformer and 30 feet of train wire to remotely heat a match head buried within the tube, which would ignite the powder when the train transformer was switched on. Sure enough, it worked! Boom!

After setting off a dozen or so of these tubes in my back yard and becoming bored, I thought if I varied the formula of the powder, I could get more bang for the volume of the tube, which I successfully did. My dad finally ended these experiments after he felt that I was about to cross the boundary where my experiments were no longer safe. This of course could never happen today without the police and Department of Homeland Security taking an intense interest. The times we live in today has taken away the freedom of kids to explore, and just be kids.

At the age of 15, I was fortunate to have the opportunity to work for Sylvan Pools in the company's retail store in Jenkintown, PA, selling swimming pool supplies to customers during the summer months. My uncle Herman Silverman was the founder and CEO of Sylvan Pools, at the time the largest pool company in the eastern part of the United States.

While working for the company during the summer for three years, I developed a work ethic and learned how to interact with our customers to meet their needs. The phrase "delivering a great customer experience" was not in usage at the time, but in retrospect, that is what the store manager taught me to do. Reflecting back, these summers at Sylvan Pools provided invaluable experience and helped develop my interpersonal skills.

While attending Drexel University as an undergrad chemical engineering student, I was able to pay my tuition from earnings during my three six-month co-op periods working at Thiokol Chemical Corporation, Sun Oil Company, and Sinclair Refining Company. These experiences prepared me for my professional career after graduation from Drexel.

During my 18 months of co-op experience working in industry while an undergraduate, I realized that I wanted to rise up through business management versus engineering management, so I could participate in the operational and eventually the strategic decisions impacting the companies I would work for.

After earning a Bachelor of Science degree in chemical engineering, I went back to Drexel to earn an MBA part-time. The most impactful part of my graduate business education was the independent project I undertook building a Monte-Carlo computer simulation model written in Fortran 4 on punch cards to evaluate the attractiveness of investment alternatives. I spent an extra year as an MBA student to build this model.

The logic I learned by writing this computer program (this was prior to the availability of apps—you had to write your own software!) and what I learned about how to financially justify capital projects and present them to the board for approval had an important influence on my career.

These were the days when each line of program instruction was typed on a punch-card. I carried 2,000 of these cards around in a box. The software was run on an IBM 360 mainframe computer, where I might get two or three runs of the program each day. The state of writing software has certainly changed over the years!

Professional Journey

After graduating from Drexel, I worked as a process engineer for Atlantic Richfield at the company's Philadelphia oil refinery. Even though I worked in engineering, I was exposed to the economics of how refineries operated. This experience and the mindset I developed proved to be very valuable in subsequent positions during my career working at PQ Corporation, which developed catalysts for the refining and petrochemical industries.

After working two years at Atlantic Richfield, the company announced a massive restructuring of its Philadelphia refinery, and I was told I would eventually be relocated to one of the other refineries within the company. My wife and I had just purchased a new home and wanted to know from the company if we should back out of the purchase.

With no response from the company, I decided to search for another job and went to work as a process engineer for privately held Philadelphia Quartz Company, later renamed PQ Corporation. Little did I know that this change in employer would send me on a trajectory through 11 positions at PQ. The experience gained at these positions and a track record of success would eventually allow me to attain the position of PQ's chief executive officer.

I never planned to stay at PQ, but I kept on getting promoted to positions that included manager of operations planning, product manager, marketing manager, sales manager, and president of PQ's Canadian subsidiary in Toronto. Three years later, I was again promoted and moved back to corporate headquarters in Valley Forge, PA, as president of PQ's global industrial chemicals group.

Shortly after my appointment to this global leadership position, I attended the three-month Advance Management Program at the Harvard Business School, where senior leaders from around the world worked on business case studies and exchanged views on different approaches to complex business problems. This was a very valuable experience.

I was subsequently promoted to the position of executive vice president and chief operating officer and in January 2000, I was named by the board of PQ as the company's chief executive officer.

For five years, I served as PQ's CEO, leading this global chemical, catalyst, and engineered glass materials company operating in 19 countries with 56 plant locations around the world. During this time, earnings grew from $14 million (adjusted for an adverse material competitive situation) to $43 million over the five years that included 9/11 and the severe recession of 2002. After 2000, we never had a down quarter. As measured by revenues growth, earnings growth, and return on assets, we moved from fourth quartile performance to first quartile performance, compared with 17 public peer companies within the chemical industry.

I didn't drive our revenues and earnings growth; the talented men and women within the company did so. As the CEO, all I did was set the tone at the top, nurtured the proper culture, espoused our values, developed overall strategy with my team, selected the right leaders reporting to me, empowered them, and then cut them loose to do their thing.

When PQ was sold in February 2005 to a private equity investor, I stepped down as CEO to begin my second career as a corporate director, serving on public, private, private equity, and nonprofit boards, including chairman of the board of the Drexel University College of Medicine and vice chairman of the Drexel board. Nine years later, I started my third career, writing for *Philadelphia Business Journal* and sharing what I have learned about how leadership builds successful businesses. Through my company Silverman Leadership, I started speaking at numerous business conferences and coaching C-suite executives as well as college students preparing to start their careers.

During my career, I challenged company policies that I thought didn't make sense and occasionally made decisions that violated policy for the good of the company. Fortunately, I was celebrated and not terminated. Sometimes, it's best to ask for forgiveness rather than permission. I have made mistakes and experienced failures, but that did not discourage me from moving forward.

I have learned you need to get out of your comfort zone, take advantage of opportunities that come your way, and create your own opportunities. You never know where the future will take you and what you can achieve.

I write about my experiences and observations as a way of giving back to those who have gone before me and helped me be successful, and to make a difference in the lives of others. For me, helping others be successful is one of the most satisfying things anyone can do.

I write to share advice with my two sons Rob and Eric and my daughters-in-law Ali and Rachel, as they continue to develop their careers. My articles will be there as a source of advice to my four grandchildren, Andrew, Lauren, Aidan, and Sydney Ruth. I never knew my great-grand-parents and feel a loss at not knowing who they were. By writing, my great grandchildren will know who I am. All they need to do is Google my name.

My objective is to help businesses thrive and provide guidance to individuals, so they become more effective leaders, entrepreneurs, and board members. I am paying it forward. This is my legacy. I hope those who follow me do the same.

Introduction

This book is about how businesses and individuals pursuing their careers can achieve success by being different.

The fundamental goal of any business is to be different—to be better than those with whom it is competing. Every company should be on a journey to be the preferred provider of products or services to its markets by offering a great customer/client experience. A preferred provider is the company that customers and clients preferentially want to do business with, and often can charge a premium for what they provide.

The fundamental goal of any individual is to be different—to be better their peers, than those with whom they are competing for that next job, whether internally or externally at a new company. Their goal is to demonstrate to the hiring manager that they are the best choice for that position. I often ask the people I counsel: How will you differentiate yourself from the 100 other applicants for the job to which you are applying? Being different is how you win your next job.

Much of the content of this book has been taken from the more than 270 columns I have written for American City Business Journals and its subsidiary, *Philadelphia Business Journal* since 2014. I hope that what I have written will help you become better at what you do, build competitive advantage for your organizations to become preferred providers to your markets, advance in your career, and become successful and recognized leaders in your fields.

This book consists of 64 chapters organized into four parts. The chapters do not need to be read sequentially, so you can read those that are of immediate interest, and other chapters more leisurely.

If you are interested in reading my articles published in the *Business Journal,* you can access them at my website: *http://silvermanleadership .com/category/articles/*

PART 1

The Importance of Leadership to Building a Thriving Business

CHAPTER 1-1

What Makes an Effective Leader?

Figure 1-1 Setting the right tone at the top and nurturing the right culture are fundamental to any organization's success.

Photo: Warchi Collection/Getty Images

I have worked for some very effective leaders who have inspired me and my colleagues to achieve beyond expectations. I have also worked for so-called leaders who were not very effective. I have learned much from both. Thinking about my experiences, effective leaders have the following characteristics. They:

Set the Tone at the Top and Nurture the Right Culture

CEOs set the tone at the top, which embodies the organization's ethical standards. CEOs nurture the institutional culture, which are the values by which employees conduct the business of the organization as well as interact with each other and the firm's stakeholders. I believe setting the right tone at the top and nurturing the right culture are fundamental to any organization's success.

Management consultant Christie Lindor writes, "People do not just quit companies or leaders … they quit organizational cultures."[1] An organizational culture can run the gamut—from benign to a toxic cut-throat culture where some employees undermine their colleagues and throw them under the bus in an attempt to eliminate the competition for the next promotion.

CEOs, ensure that you and the leaders below you within the organization set the right tone and nurture the right culture. If tone and culture aren't right, you are apt to lose your high performing employees, perhaps to a competitor. In today's tough business environment, you can ill afford to lose them. Boards, include tone and culture in your CEO's performance review. More on tone and culture throughout this book.

Have a High Degree of Emotional Intelligence

In a 2004 *Harvard Business Review* article, "Leading by Feel,"[2] University of New Hampshire psychologist John D. Mayer wrote, "Emotional intelligence is the ability to accurately perceive your own and others' emotions; to understand the signals that emotions send about relationships; and to manage your own and others' emotions."

I agree with Meyers, based on personal experience working with peers and for bosses as I rose up through the organization to the position of CEO, serving in leadership rolls and as a board member observing other CEOs. I will go into more detail about the elements of emotional intelligence in Chapter 1-2.

---

[1] https://linkedin.com/pulse/people-do-quit-companies-managers-leaders-cultures-heres-lindor/

[2] https://hbr.org/2004/01/leading-by-feel

Communicate the Vision and Mission of the Organization

Effective leaders have a vision of what they want their company to become and the mission they want their company to fulfill and have a strategic sense of how to get there. They communicate with all employees the vision and mission, and the role the employees will play in achieving them.

Choose the Right Leadership Team

Effective leaders surround themselves with the team that will help make the vision and mission a reality and inspire their team to achieve them. They challenge each other's paradigms and to think out of the box. The team helps further define the vision and mission and participates in setting goals. When all team members feel a sense of ownership in achieving the vision and mission, there is a high probability that they will be achieved.

They are focused on achieving results through others and understand that having the right people on the team is of critical importance for success. Effective leaders understand that the vision and mission cannot be achieved without people who have common sense and good critical judgment.

Embrace Continuous Improvement and Encourage a Sense of Ownership in Employees

Effective leaders know how to achieve operational excellence, and they embrace continuous improvement. They inspire their direct reports and nurture an environment in which their people develop a sense of ownership in what they do.

These leaders never micromanage. They let their people do their jobs and hold them accountable for results. They ensure their people have access to both the financial and human resources they need to get the job done.

Are Always on a Journey to Become a Great Company

How many of you have heard leaders refer to their organization as great? This is for third parties to decide, not them. Once you think you are great, you have nowhere to go but down. Every organization should always be on a journey to achieve greatness. It's a journey that never ends.

Encourage Meaningful Communication

Create an environment where your employees are comfortable speaking with you. By doing so, you will learn more about what is going on in your organization, which will help you achieve the organization's goals.

Some CEOs act in an imperial manner. This style separates them from the employees they are leading and hurts their employees' ability to relate to them.

As a leader, listen to your employees and create an environment in which they are comfortable telling you what they think. Earn their respect and trust. You will be a more effective leader when you relate to your employees and they relate to you.

Acknowledge the Work of Direct Reports

A number of individuals have shared with me that their work is rarely acknowledged when passed up through the organization. I personally experienced this when I was told that all work leaving our department had to have the name of the department's manager on it, rather than a cover letter transmitting the work of a direct report. I knew that this was not the kind of manager I wanted to work for.

In another instance, I was told by the creator of an advertising campaign of an experience she had after she presented her work during a meeting with a client. The client loved the campaign. After the presentation, she was not invited to join her boss and the client at a lunch celebrating the campaign's creation. Why was her boss tone-deaf and insensitive to how that made her feel? This is not the way to inspire and motivate direct reports.

Respect All Colleagues, Whether Male or Female

I have heard from many women that they are still not as respected as men within the workplace. In many cases, this is not purposeful, but part of an ingrained cultural norm.

A company with an organizational culture that tolerates a hostile work environment or doesn't respect both men and women signals to some current and potential employees that they are not welcome and valued. The recent #MeToo movement has shined a light on the issue of sexual harassment in the workplace and it hopefully indicates the start of a cultural change.

All organizations should create a respectful work environment and provide advancement opportunities to all employees based upon their skills and track record of accomplishments. This should be part of the cultural norm of the company, driven by the CEO. If this is not a cultural norm, eventually the reputation of the organization will be damaged. Boards, ensure your CEO drives this cultural norm.

Effective leaders are inspirational and great role models. Count yourself fortunate when you work for one. You will learn much. As you develop and refine your leadership style, be sure to carefully and intentionally choose the leaders you surround yourself with. When you seek out those who have truly earned the title of leader, your own journey to the top will be richly enhanced.

CHAPTER 1-2

Emotional Intelligence Is a Key Leadership Trait

Is emotional intelligence (emotional quotient, EQ) more important than IQ in one's success? Are street smarts more important than book smarts?

In a 1998 *Harvard Business Review* article headlined, "What Makes a Leader?"[3] Rutgers University professor Daniel Goleman wrote,

The most effective leaders are alike in one crucial way: They all have a high degree of what has come to be known as emotional intelligence. It's not that IQ and technical skills are irrelevant. They do matter, but mainly as "threshold capabilities"; that is, they are the entry-level requirements for executive positions.

But my research, along with other recent studies, clearly shows that emotional intelligence is the *sine qua non of l*eadership. Without it, a person can have the best training in the world, an incisive, analytical mind, and an endless supply of smart ideas, but he [/she] still won't make a great leader.

In his article, Goleman identifies five components of EQ:

Self-awareness: The ability to recognize and understand your moods, emotions and drives, as well as their effect on others.
Self-regulation: The ability to control or redirect disruptive impulses and moods ... to think before acting.

---

[3] https://hbr.org/product/what-makes-a-leader-hbr-bestseller/R0401H-PDF-ENG

Motivation: A passion to work for reasons that go beyond money or status.

Empathy: The ability to understand the emotional makeup of other people. Skill in treating people according to their emotional reactions.

Social Skill: Proficiency in managing relationships and building networks. An ability to find common ground and build rapport.

How do these five components of EQ translate into a leader's day-to-day interactions and effectiveness with the people they deal with? I would like to share with you, based on my experience interacting with others, seven EQ behavioral rules that will contribute to your leadership effectiveness.

Don't Ever Undermine Your Relationship with Your Allies

Only people who lack emotional intelligence do this. They need you and you need them. What do you think their reaction will be when you criticize them in public?

Recognize How Others Perceive You

You should perceive how your words, body language, verbal tone, and actions are read by others. If the way you are being read is not the way you desire or is ineffective, you should change. You can tell how you are being perceived by other people's subtle or not-so-subtle cues.

When making a verbal statement or writing an e-mail, always consider how the tone and content of your message will be received. Control how you are viewed by the people you communicate with and how you influence them. Understand the impact of your spoken and written word.

Always Use Your Common Sense and Good Critical Judgment

Most decisions are made with only a limited amount of data, so you need to fall back on your common sense and good critical judgment. Be sure to use them. Ensure you hire people with these two traits. There are too many examples of employees causing economic and reputational harm to the company because they lacked them.

Don't Communicate with Others in a Way That Puts Them on the Defensive

Communicate in a way so people feel respected and valued. Don't criticize others in public or undermine them. If you need to give them negative feedback, do so in private. Don't waste your personal capital correcting individuals on minor irrelevant misstatements of fact. If a correction is necessary, do it in a way so that the individual maintains their dignity and you are not showing how smart you are.

I once worked with a colleague who would put others on the defensive when they changed their position while discussing a still undecided issue, especially when the change was counter to his own position. He would say "That's not the position you had yesterday!" in an attempt to intimidate the individual to continue to support his own position. Not a great way to build trust.

When a Direct Report Shares an Idea or Proposes a New Initiative, Listen

Don't accept or reject an idea out of hand before vetting it. Show respect by discussing the idea with the direct report, asking them questions on how it might be implemented, its impact, and if there could be any unintended consequences.

It's better to have them reach their own conclusion through dialogue rather than you prematurely telling them what you think. After a dialogue, both of you might have new positions or discover an alternative that is more effective than the original idea.

Value the opinion of the lone wolf within your organization. It takes courage and conviction to go against the grain. Give them a chance to air their views. They might just change your mind.

Take the Blame If It's Your Fault. Give Credit Where Credit Is Due

Everyone makes mistakes. Own up to yours. You will be a much more effective and respected leader if you do. Publicly acknowledge the successes of others. It will motivate them to continue to succeed. And, never throw people under the bus. It destroys trust and any respect people within your organization might have for you.

People Don't Like To Be Bullied

Making threats to people to get what you want rarely works. It strengthens their resolve. There are more effective ways to meet your objectives while maintaining good relationships, which is to your advantage in future interactions. People have long memories, and you may need their support in the future.

Don't Self-Aggrandize

Avoid telling everyone how great you are compared to your predecessors. Don't blame them for decisions you disagree with for the purpose of boosting your own perceived standing. Narcissistic, insecure people do this. It does nothing to win the hearts and minds and earn the respect of your organization and the other people you deal with. It makes you look bad.

The skills outlined in this chapter are referred to by many as soft skills. They are not. Quoting Donna De Carolis, founding dean of the Charles D. Close School of Entrepreneurship at Drexel Univesity, they are power skills. They differentiate you from your peers.

Practice street smarts. Lead like you would like to be led and treat people like you would like to be treated. Follow these emotional intelligence rules for leadership and business success.

CHAPTER 1-3

Set the Right Tone at the Top and Nurture the Right Organizational Culture

When boards evaluate the annual performance of their CEOs, the areas assessed are most often focused on those metrics that drive shareholder value, such as growth in revenues, cash flow and earnings, as well as annual and multiyear operational and strategic goals. Goals are established by the board and the CEO at the beginning of the year; and at the end of the year, results are measured against those established goals.

Evaluated less often are leadership traits of the CEO. Unlike performance against numerical goals, these are more subjective and harder to assess, but very important to the long-term success of the company. The assessment of the following traits should be part of every CEO performance review.

Sets the Right Tone at the Top and Corporate Culture

The importance of tone at the top and corporate culture cannot be overestimated for the long-term success of any organization.

In today's world where social media can adversely impact the reputation of a company, a tone needs to be established where the company and its employees will do the right thing. The last thing any CEO wants is to appear in the news media in the wrong light.

Tone at the top is the ethical compass of the company. Corporate culture is the environment in which employees are treated and deal with each other. The firms where employees are held to high ethical and performance standards and are treated with respect will outperform those that don't. These firms become an employer of choice and attract the best employees.

Corporate culture also determines how customers and clients are treated. Those companies that listen to and exceed the expectations of their customers differentiate themselves. They create a competitive advantage and can become preeminent in their industry. Those companies that are arrogant toward their customers hand their competitors a significant competitive advantage. At PQ Corporation, as CEO and while serving in prior sales, marketing, and other executive leadership positions, we won significant business going up against arrogant competitors.

Establishes a Clear Vision and Mission for the Organization

If you don't know where you are going, you can't get there, and without a clear vision and mission, the long-term goals of operating and staff units down through the organization will not be aligned.

The process of establishing a clear vision and mission should involve the senior leadership team, so the team develops a sense of ownership and commitment to the vision and mission so they can communicate this role down through their respective units.

Encourages Team Cohesiveness, Maximizing the Results of the Whole Organization

Organizations with cohesive teams that operate to maximize the results of the organization as a whole will outperform organizations where members of the senior leadership team are only interested in the performance of their own respective unit. These organizations tend to be siloed. Employees within each unit will sense the importance that the CEO and the leader of their unit places on cohesiveness and will behave accordingly.

Develops Strong Leaders

One of the prime responsibilities of the CEO is to develop strong leaders and a strong leadership team. I have served on boards where the leadership team below the CEO was weak. The market served by the company was growing, but the leadership team was not capable of delivering results, and the company underperformed its peers. It is the job of the CEO to ensure all direct reports are strong leaders in their own right, and that they, in turn, are developing leaders within their respective units.

Is Transparent with the Board

CEOs that are transparent with their boards engender trust. No one likes surprises—not the CEO and certainly not the company's directors. CEOs earn respect by sharing problems and issues with their boards and outline how these will be addressed. Directors can offer advice, but it is up to the CEO to choose the right path forward.

Directors are an important resource to CEOs, and CEOs should seek their input. Effective CEOs are transparent with their directors. Only when the brutal facts of reality are recognized and discussed can problems be effectively addressed.

The above traits should be part of all CEO performance reviews, not only for the purpose of assessing performance, but also to provide critical feedback to the CEO to reinforce areas of strength, as well as point out areas for improvement. Everyone is on a journey to improve, and it is the job of the board to help further develop its CEO.

CHAPTER 1-4

Always Lead Your Organization with the Highest Level of Ethics and Integrity

Scandals at the Philadelphia Parking Authority and at the Philadelphia Housing Authority are teachable moments in what happens when the CEO doesn't lead their organization with the highest levels of ethics and integrity, and boards don't adopt the best governance practices and don't hold the CEO accountable to the highest standards of behavior.

Philadelphia Parking Authority Scandal

In a decision on September 27, 2016, the board of the Philadelphia Parking Authority allowed its then executive director, Vincent Fenerty, to keep his job after an investigation showed that he had sexually harassed an employee. The board reduced his personnel decision-making power, imposed other restrictions, and made him pay the $30,000 charged by an outside investigator working on the case. How could the board possibly think Fenerty could continue to be effective as executive director?

Felicia Harris, president of Philadelphia Commission on Women, said, "[Fenerty's] continued employment sends the message that sexual harassment is OK,[4] and that the harm caused can be erased by monetary payment. Sexual harassment can't be written off like a parking fine."

Shortly after the decision by the Parking Authority to permit Fenerty to remain in his position, the board learned that he sexually harassed

---

[4] https://philly.com/philly/news/politics/20160923_Councilmembers_challenge_Parking_Authority_on_director_s_sexual_harassment_of_coworker.html

another employee in 2006. Fenerty resigned on September 28, 2016, knowing that this time the board would fire him.

The 2006 sexual harassment accusation was not reported to the board by the Parking Authority's general counsel, a gross violation of good governance practices, nor did the board have the opportunity to vote on the $150,000 settlement offered to the victim, which she ultimately turned down.

Philadelphia Housing Authority Scandal

In a scandal at the Philadelphia Housing Authority, executive director Carl Greene settled four sexual harassment claims over five years[5] by paying off the victims and not telling his board he was doing so. Greene faced similar accusations in the past, but the board members hired him anyway. Greene also faced a host of corruption accusations, which resulted in a federal investigation. He was fired on September 23, 2010.

Describing the culture within the Philadelphia Housing Authority under Greene's leadership as "toxic" is an understatement. Where was the board while all this was going on?

Do all governmental authority organizations have hotlines directly to the audit committees of their boards for employees to report wrongdoing by leaders or the organization? Will the audit committee of the board take appropriate action against wrongdoers? Even if hotlines are in place, do employees believe that they won't face retaliation if they use the hotline?

These are not only best governance practices in public companies and in many private companies and nonprofit organizations, they are common practices. Why is anything less tolerated in some governmental authority organizations?

The most important responsibility of any board is to hire and fire the CEO, establish levels of authority beyond which he or she needs to go to the board for approval and assess his or her performance against

---

[5] https://metro.us/local/pha-ends-carl-greene-suit-with-625k-settlement/tmWmbx---3fvAL2zgUQXg

established goals. The board must also hold the CEO accountable for tone at the top and organizational culture.

Scandals occur in organizations in which tone at the top and culture are poor. These scandals are often reported on the front pages of the local or national press, damaging the reputations of the organization, its leader, and its board members.

Qualification of Board Members

This raises the issue of the qualifications of board members of government authorities. Do they know how to be effective board members? Are they selected purely on their political connections or by patronage considerations, or are they chosen for their specific functional experience and expertise?

No employee should have to work in an organization in which ethical lapses or illegal activities occur, nor where employees lack confidence in using the hotline to report these activities. When governmental authority organizations are not operated using best governance practices, not only do the employees suffer, but the public is shortchanged as well. Both deserve better.

Lessons Taught by the Challenger Space Shuttle Disaster

Figure 1-5 Smoke from the explosion of the challenger space craft, January 28, 1986.

Photo: Dave Welcher, Getty Images.

On January 28, 1986, the space shuttle Challenger exploded 73 seconds after liftoff due to a leak in one of the O-rings of the solid rocket booster, resulting in the death of all seven crew members and the loss of the shuttle. This tragedy teaches leaders three valuable lessons:

Face the Brutal Facts of Reality and Listen to Your Experts

The engineers at Morton Thiokol, the contractor responsible for the design of the solid rocket boosters, were concerned about the cold temperature on launch day and the effect it would have on the solid rocket booster O-rings. The O-rings were designed to operate at an ambient temperature of not less than 40 degrees Fahrenheit. On the day of the launch, the ambient temperature was 30 degrees. Concerned about the brittleness of the O-rings, Thiokol told NASA that the launch needed to be postponed.

NASA objected to the recommendation to delay the launch. The launch had already been delayed a number of times for various reasons. One NASA manager is quoted as saying, "I am appalled by your recommendation."[6] Another NASA manager said, "My God, Thiokol, when do you want me to launch—next April?"[7]

In January 2016, columnist Howard Berkes wrote an article for the NPR publication *The Two-Way* headlined, "30 years after explosion, Challenger engineer still blames himself."[8] For his article, Berkes interviewed Morton Thiokol engineer Robert Ebeling, who told the story of how he and four other engineers did not want the Challenger to be launched due to cold weather conditions. In spite of their concern, NASA launched the shuttle anyway.

Ebeling told Berkes,

> I was one of the few that was really close to the situation. Had they listened to me and wait[ed] for a weather change, it might have been a completely different outcome. … [NASA] had their mind set on going up and proving to the world they were right, and they knew what they were doing. But they didn't.

After I wrote an article on the efforts of Ebeling and fellow Thiokol engineers to delay the launch of Challenger, Ebeling's daughter reached out and thanked me for recognizing her father. I asked if I might speak to him, and she shared his phone number with me. A few days later I spoke with Ebeling and told him he and his Thiokol colleagues were true American heroes for trying to delay the launch. He passed away five days later.

---

[6] https://npr.org/sections/thetwo-way/2012/02/06/146490064/remembering-roger-boisjoly-he-tried-to-stop-shuttle-challenger-launch

[7] https://npr.org/sections/thetwo-way/2016/03/21/470870426/challenger-engineer-who-warned-of-shuttle-disaster-dies

[8] https://npr.org/sections/thetwo-way/2016/01/28/464744781/30-years-after-disaster-challenger-engineer-still-blames-himself

Value the Contributions of the Lone Wolf

President Ronald Reagan established the Rogers Commission (named for its chairman Willian P. Rogers) to investigate the reasons for the Challenger disaster. The Commission found that NASA, concerned about their inability to meet an unrealistic launch schedule that might jeopardize their Congressional funding, did not face the brutal facts of their reality—launching in cold weather conditions would expose the Challenger to an unacceptably high level of O-ring failure risk.

Physicist Richard Feynman, the lone wolf on the Rogers Commission, delved further into the loss of Challenger. Feynman clearly saw that cultural issues, poor communication, and a lack of understanding of risk within NASA were major factors in the Challenger disaster.[9]

Through his own work independent of the Commission, Feynman learned that NASA management felt that the likelihood of shuttle failure was one in 100,000, compared with NASA engineers, who felt that the likelihood of failure was one in 100, a huge disconnect between management and their technical experts.

Many times, a decision will come down to assessing the risks of various courses of action. *When the possible result of a course of action is catastrophic even if the probability of it occurring is low, one should not take the risk.* Unfortunately, the NASA decision makers who moved ahead with the Challenger launch did not think in these terms. They were more worried about their unrealistic launch schedule commitment to Congress.

When Feynman learned that the final Commission report would not focus on the issues he felt were key to the loss of the shuttle, he decided to write a minority report. If it wasn't for Feynman, these issues within NASA might not have been identified and addressed, perhaps leading to future shuttle disasters.

Nurture a Challenge Culture—An Imperative for All Organizations

How many times have you sat in a meeting in which not one of the attendees challenged the prevailing opinion about the issue being discussed?

---

[9] http://ralentz.com/old/space/feynman-report.html

What is it about an organizational culture that prevents at least one lone wolf independent thinker from expressing a counter opinion? Does the leader voice a negative reaction to a counter opinion, rather than encourage the attendees to speak their minds?

In his book, *The Challenge Culture: Why Most Successful Organizations Run on Pushback*,[10] former chairman and CEO of Dunkin Brands Group Nigel Travis writes about the importance of establishing a challenge culture within organizations in which input from employees is welcomed.

Travis writes that a challenge culture is one "in which direct reports can challenge their bosses … and colleagues can challenge each other… [so that] people have a say, where people understand what's going on. The results are great business solutions and total buy-in, because people feel involved [and respected]."

Of course, that culture needs to focus on attacking business issues and not people, so that challenging others doesn't destroy working relationships. Respecting civil discourse is a key determinant for success in a challenge culture.

Working in a challenge culture requires individuals with the self-confidence to hear criticism of their ideas and not take it personally, and to have the ability to challenge others.

Leaders, create an environment and institutional culture that welcomes and encourages individuals to share their opinions. A courageous independent thinker should feel comfortable voicing their opinion and try to convince everyone of the validity of the organization's reality. The views of the independent thinker may not be ultimately adopted, but at a minimum, those views provide a different path, a path against which the majority opinion can be tested and either confirmed or changed. Under this type of process, the best decisions will emerge.

In the words of renowned Brazilian novelist, Paulo Coelho, "If you want to be successful, you must respect one rule: Never lie to yourself." Leaders, remember this when one of the independent thinkers on your staff reminds you to face the brutal facts of your reality.

---

[10] https://amazon.com/Challenge-Culture-Successful-Organizations-Pushback/dp/1541762142

CHAPTER 1-6

How to Earn Employees' Trust and Build a High-Performance Team

Have you ever worked in an organization where there was a low level of trust among peers or where direct reports did not trust their boss or the CEO of the company? This type of organization has a toxic atmosphere, which significantly reduces its effectiveness and its ability to achieve results.

What is "trust"? The Merriam-Webster dictionary defines trust as a "belief that someone is reliable, good, honest and effective ... one in which confidence is placed." Wouldn't we all like to work within organizations in which all employees feel this level of trust in their leaders and peers?

Stephen Covey, the late motivational speaker, writer, and advisor, once wrote, "Without trust we don't truly collaborate; we merely coordinate or, at best, cooperate. It is trust that transforms a group of people into a team."[11] When people don't trust each other, there is an invisible elephant in the room, which may adversely impact the effectiveness of any decision.

Whether you are the CEO, a mid-level manager, or an individual contributor with no direct reports but a member of a team, trust needs to be earned. So, how do you earn the trust of others?

---

[11] https://mwaexeccoach.wordpress.com/2016/03/02/trust/

Be Consistent and Readable by Those Within Your Organization

As a leader, there should be no misunderstanding as to the tone and culture you embrace. These reflect the values to which you hold yourself and your employees accountable. *Employees trust and want to be part of an organization with high ethical standards and work for a leader that lives by those standards.*

As the leader, ensure your expectations are understood. Situations will arise when decisions need to be made by your employees for which there is no operating procedure or precedent. Employees will fall back on their common sense and good critical judgment, and proceed in a way consistent with your expectations, tone, and culture.

Learn to Effectively Work with Those Within Your Group

Get to know your co-workers and peers on a personal level, in addition to a professional level. Be genuine. Take an interest in them. Be supportive and collaborative with what they do. Treat them as valued and respected colleagues. Sense how they view you and change your behavior if you sense you are not being accepted. There are few things worse than feeling like an outsider or not trusted by those in your group.

Meet Your Commitments

Don't make a commitment you cannot keep. If the situation changes and you find that you can't keep a commitment, notify the individual who you made the commitment to immediately. They may have made a commitment to others, based on your commitment to them.

Don't Blame Other People for Your Mistakes

If you make a mistake, own it and share how in the future the issue will be handled in a different manner. You don't create trust by blaming others for your mistake. Employees that do this never last long within the kind of organization in which we all want to work.

Listen!

Focus on what others are saying. Listen intently. Ask questions for understanding. Maintain an appropriate amount of eye contact. If your gaze drifts, you send a signal that you are not interested in what an individual is saying. If they are perceptive, they will stop talking to you. Make them feel that you are genuinely interested in what they have to say, even if you don't agree with them.

Allow Your Direct Reports to Share with You a Contrary Point of View

I have worked for bosses who were not interested in contrary views. This did not engender trust. As the leader, compare their opinion on how to proceed on an issue with your own view. Through discussion and debate, you may accept their view or may discover a third alternative path, better than either of the first two paths. Follow this process, and you will rarely choose the wrong way to proceed.

Create an Environment That Allows Employees to Share the Brutal Facts of Reality

As a leader, you want your people to feel safe in sharing bad news. Don't shoot the messenger. You can't solve a problem unless you know what it is. You want your people to have trust and confidence that you will listen to them.

Help Employees Develop a Sense of Ownership in What They Do

Empower employees, don't micromanage. Show your employees that you trust them by letting them decide how to accomplish an objective. This will help your employees develop a sense of ownership in what they do. When this occurs, you can rely on them to drive results.

This lesson was taught to me as president of PQ Corporation's Canadian subsidiary by an hourly worker, Luigi Paolini, who was given the responsibility of developing the scope and managing the expansion of his production unit at our Toronto plant. The project was executed flawlessly. After startup of the expansion, I was taking a visitor through the plant and about to give the visitor a tour of Paolini's newly expanded unit. Paolini stopped me and insisted that he conduct the tour.

The next day, Paolini asked me if I knew why he insisted on conducting the tour for the visitor. When I shook my head, Paolini said, "This is my production unit, not yours." By trusting Paolini to develop and execute the scope of the expansion, we helped him develop a sense of ownership in what he did at the company. During the ensuing months, every performance metric of the production unit improved under Paolini's newly developed feeling of ownership.

The lesson taught to me by Paolini helped me fundamentally change my leadership focus for the rest of my career. Nurture a culture in which employees can develop a sense of ownership in what they do.

Be Accessible and Transparent

Create opportunities for employees other than your direct reports to talk with you. Walk around the office or factory floor. Ask how people are doing. However, avoid telling them what to do. Don't violate the chain of command. If you learn of an issue that needs to be addressed, talk with your direct report responsible for the area. Hold town meetings to talk about the business and respond to employees' questions. Be as transparent as possible, realizing that there are things that cannot be publicly shared.

Before Making a Decision, Hear Both Sides of an Issue

No matter how compelling an argument is presented by an individual, there is always the other side, which may be more compelling. Hear both sides before making a decision. The individual on the losing side of the issue won't like your decision but will respect the fact that you went through a fair decision-making process.

Live Your Values

Living your values engenders trust. As CEO of PQ, I experienced a minor OSHA recordable accident while traveling on business. I insisted that the accident be written up, and for that quarter, I was one of PQ's safety statistics. Word was spread to our 56 manufacturing facilities around the world that the CEO called an OSHA recordable accident on himself. This demonstrated that I held myself accountable to the same standards as I held our employees.

The best talent will want to work for companies where there are high levels of trust with the senior leadership as well as among fellow employees and where employees feel a sense of ownership in what they do. These are the companies that have the lowest turnover and achieve the highest long-term returns to shareholders. This is the type of company at which we all want to work.

To Improve Your Effectiveness, Relate to Your Employees

Much has been written about the characteristics of effective leaders. One of these characteristics is a leader's ability to relate to their employees, as well as act in a way so that their employees can relate to them.

Relate to Employees

When situations arise that permit your employees to relate to you, take advantage of the moment. I recall the day I held a town hall meeting at one of our plants two days after we announced the shutdown of one of the plant's production units, resulting in the layoff of 17 hourly production and maintenance employees. As then chief operating officer of PQ Corporation, I wanted to explain that the shutdown was a result of a large customer exiting one of their businesses, and therefore they no longer required the product produced by that production unit.

To say the attendees at the town meeting were not very happy would be an understatement. At a tense moment, one of the hourly workers said to me, "What do you know about working in a chemical plant? All you do is sit behind a desk all day, push paper, and make decisions that affect our lives." My immediate response was, "When I was a co-op student at Drexel University on an industry assignment, I worked as an hourly employee in a plant like this one and learned much from the production and maintenance staff, so I do know what it's like to work in a chemical plant."

I earned instant credibility with those hourly workers, because I related to them in a very effective manner. I was once one of them. The tense atmosphere in the meeting was instantly diffused.

Allow Yourself To Be Read by Your Employees

Have you ever worked for a boss that you could not "read" or who didn't communicate the direction they wanted to pursue, leaving you wondering how you should proceed on an issue? As a leader, allow yourself to be read by your employees. If you have not yet decided on a course of action, be open about it and ask for input, which will help guide you to the best decision.

Create an environment where your employees are comfortable speaking with you. By doing so, you will learn more about what is going on in your organization, which will help you achieve the organization's goals.

Never Act in an Imperial Manner

An imperial CEO can hurt the ability for their employees to relate to them. When promoted from chief operating officer to CEO, I faced many challenges to earnings growth, requiring organizational changes and reductions in staff. I chose to remain in my row office and not move into my predecessor's corner office. I converted the corner office into a reception area open to all employees where we could meet with visitors to our company. I did not upgrade my car to a more expensive model.

These were symbols to our employees that my priority was not me, but to grow the company and increase shareholder value. As CEO, I valued the willingness of my employees to share with me what was on their mind. They were comfortable in doing so because I was not viewed as an imperial CEO.

So, as a leader, listen to your employees and create an environment where they are comfortable telling you what they think. Don't act like an imperial leader. Earn their respect and trust. You will be a more effective leader when you relate to your employees and they relate to you.

The ABCs of Decision Making

Figure 1-8 The best solutions come from debating an issue.

Photo: Fizkes Collection/Getty Images

Have you ever worked for a leader who would not listen to your ideas? This type of boss saps the energy out of the organization. Employees turn off any desire to work more effectively, don't go the extra mile for their customers, and put less than their best efforts into growing the business. This creates an undesirable working environment, and the best and brightest employees won't stick around for long.

Be Open to the Opinions of Your Employees

As a young leader, I adopted an open culture with my direct reports that encouraged them to share their opinion and input on any issue, and I expected that they in turn would do the same with their direct reports.

I utilized the ABCs of decision making in order to come up with the best solution to an issue, relying on input from those employees with experience and expertise.

In my subsequent leadership roles including that of CEO, I would normally ask for opinions on an issue before I shared my own ideas. However, on occasion, I might first propose that we go with solution A on a certain issue. Within our culture, a member of the senior leadership team might share their view that solution B might be the better option. The manner in which I communicated my response would convey how welcome their opinion was, and this would affect their desire to share their opinion on this issue and future issues.

My approach would be to ask why they thought B was a better option than A. We would then discuss the alternatives for an hour, a day, or however long was appropriate. We would also invite other employees with expertise on the subject and those with good critical judgment to join the discussion. All opinions were considered and valued before I made the final decision.

The best solutions come from debating an issue. This process would result in one of three outcomes:

1. I might sustain solution A and thank the senior leader for suggesting solution B, and for creating the opportunity for solution A to be rigorously tested against an alternative.

2. If it became apparent that solution B was the better choice after being compared against solution A, I would choose B, thank the senior leader for suggesting it, and make sure they got credit for providing the best solution. They would feel empowered because their insights were valued and their solution was chosen. They would also have a sense of ownership in the solution because they proposed it.

3. More often than not, however, by going through this process, solution C would emerge—a completely different solution or some amalgamation of A and B—which was far better than the alternatives. This outcome occurred only because we had an open culture that encouraged employees to propose alternatives and work collaboratively to determine the best solution.

When we followed this process, we always felt confident that we had made the best decision, and indeed, we found that we rarely made a mistake.

Every employee wants their voice to be heard, to feel valued, and have ownership in the decision-making process. The leaders who understand this and empower their employees to be active contributors will set themselves apart with better decision making and higher employee retention.

Remember the ABCs of decision making. Your employees will feel engaged and your organization will achieve better results.

Don't Micromanage Employees. Empower and Hold Them Accountable for Results

I often hear from many people about micromanagement issues within their respective organizations. They complain about how some bosses micromanage and make decisions that should be the responsibility of direct reports. In addition, I hear about staff units that exercise unproductive and detailed oversight on the work done by line units and other staff units that add no value.

Effective Leaders Don't Micromanage Their Direct Reports

They set goals and expectations and then empower and hold direct reports accountable for results.

Have your direct reports write the first draft of their own goals so they have ownership in them. This will enable you to get a sense of what your direct reports want to accomplish over the short and long term. You can then share what goals you want them to accomplish. Periodically, progress toward the goals should be reviewed to determine if they are on track or what corrective actions need to be taken, if appropriate.

Levels of Authority Need To Be Established

Ensure that the signature authority level for direct reports is not so low that it amounts to micromanagement. This even applies at the CEO level.

I once joined a board of a company where most capital expenditure projects went to the board for approval. This took time and focus of the board away from larger capital expenditure projects and strategic issues. The board raised the capital spending authority level of the CEO to a more appropriate level, creating time for the directors to focus on more important areas.

By micromanaging employees, you deprive them not only of the opportunity to learn, but to also feel accountable for decisions they make. Employees who do not feel accountable for their decisions will not grow in their jobs.

Occasionally, employees may need to make a decision that is within their authority level. However, the decision involves high risk or could have a reputational or strategic impact on the company. In these cases, employees should consult with their boss, or any other individual who has experience or expertise in the area. Through this process, the risk/reward profile of the decision can be better understood, and ways can be found to de-risk the decision.

This is one of the reasons among many that you should always hire people with common sense and good critical judgment. Even though a decision may be within the authority level of an individual, they need to sense when to get input from others before making the decision. Asking for other people's opinions is a strength, not a weakness.

Why do some bosses micromanage? They themselves might be micromanaged by their boss, who expects them to have all the answers, regardless of how insignificant the issue. This is a sign of poor and ineffective leadership and a poor organizational culture.

Steve Jobs once said, "We don't hire smart people to tell them what to do. We hire smart people so they can tell us what to do." When employees are micromanaged, the organization is deprived of its creativity. The best people eventually leave. The mediocre people stay, reducing the performance of the organization.

To Give Employees the Best Chance to Grow, Push Them Outside of Their Comfort Zone

An important responsibility of every leader is to develop future leaders for their organization. One of the most effective ways to do this is to push your direct reports outside of their comfort zone. Give them challenging assignments in areas that they have never faced to broaden their experience and see how they perform. Expose your employees to new meaningful experiences. There is no better way for them to develop.

My Own Experience Getting Outside My Comfort Zone

The benefits of stepping out of my comfort zone was a lesson I learned early in my career as PQ Corporation's business manager for anhydrous sodium metasilicate (ASM), which is used in a variety of metal cleaning and other industrial applications. It was also a lesson for the senior leadership of my company in the further development of a mid-level manager who eventually became CEO of the company.

We faced import competition for ASM from Rhone Poulenc, a large French chemical and pharmaceutical company, at a price significantly below their home market price in France. We felt this was a violation of U.S. dumping regulations, designed to protect U.S. industry from unfair international trade practices.

ASM producers in the United States, including my company, were losing market share. If found guilty of dumping, the remedy would be the assessment of dumping duties on imported ASM which would force Rhone Poulenc to raise their product's price.

As the business manager of this product line, I received approval from my company's CEO to file dumping charges against Rhone Poulenc with the U.S. International Trade Commission. I was 34 years old at the time, with no experience in these kinds of legal matters. However, my product manager and I knew the market well, which provided the foundation for building the case, and we both relished the challenge.

The attorney retained by our company's general counsel insisted that my product manager and I be the public face of our company's case. I soon learned what that meant.

I recall traveling to Washington, DC, for an evidentiary hearing in front of the ITC staff, asking our attorney if he was ready to provide testimony for our company. He said, "No! You are the one who is going to testify today." He said he didn't tell me ahead of time because at this hearing, he didn't want me to overprepare, but to just respond to his questioning.

It is hard for anyone to imagine the horror I felt not having written out in detail what I wanted to say. Talk about being outside of one's comfort zone! Fortunately, I knew the facts, which helped me state my company's case, despite my trepidations.

The hearing accomplished the substance of what our attorney wanted. His strategy was to pit a relatively small, privately owned, domestic company dedicated to serving the U.S. ASM market against a foreign company many times our size, competing illegally through product pricing that met the criteria of dumping.

The "Six Ps" Is a Lesson for All

One of the most lasting and valuable lessons I learned while a freshman at Drexel University was taught by my ROTC instructor, Captain Boyle. Throughout the entire course he emphasized the Six Ps: "Prior planning prevents piss-poor performance." The Six Ps certainly paid dividends in preparing our case.

The preparation for the hearing in front of the five ITC commissioners was very intense. Over a period of months, we responded to questions from the ITC investigative staff. The staff asked for significant details to ensure that the commissioners had the information needed to understand the dynamics of the market, in order to determine if dumping was occurring and if it caused harm to the U.S. domestic industry.

The credibility and trust we built with the investigative staff were important factors in the case. Whenever we realized that we had provided information to the staff that was inaccurate, we immediately corrected it, even if it hurt our case.

The hearing in front of the ITC commissioners was held in a chamber very similar to that of the Supreme Court. Somewhat intimidating!

Be Credible, Honest, and Factual

At the ITC hearing, my product manager and I were well prepared to give testimony. A pivotal moment occurred when the Rhone Poulenc attorneys misrepresented a meeting their clients had with us, accusing PQ of improper marketplace behavior. As I was listening to their mischaracterizations, I whispered to our attorney that we had notes of that meeting which countered their testimony. He asked me to pull the notes, and as he read them, a smile crossed his face.

Our meeting notes, entered into evidence, undermined much of Rhone Poulenc's credibility.

When the ITC commissioners announced their decision, they unanimously found in favor of my company and against Rhone Poulenc. They assessed the highest dumping duty on any chemical imported into the United States at that time. My product manager and I felt as if we had won gold medals at the Olympics!

So, what did we learn from this experience? Whether you are dealing with customers or the investigative staff of a federal agency, you develop credibility with those you deal with by always being honest and factual. This will differentiate you from those that aren't. Credibility builds trust and confidence, and this will favor you in borderline decisions. We also learned to operate under pressure and to get out of our comfort zone. It was a rewarding experience.

Leaders, expose your employees to new meaningful experiences. Get them out of their comfort zones. There is no better way for them to develop.

Traits to Look for When Hiring People

What are the traits business leaders should look for in employees they are hiring? Based on my own experience as a former CEO and as a board member observing the hiring practices of other leaders, I offer the following advice. Hire people who exhibit the following characteristics.

Differentiate Themselves from Their Peers

What has a job applicant accomplished in previous positions that differentiates them from other job applicants? Have they taken the initiative to do things that went beyond their job description? How have they moved the business of their previous employer forward? Are they a team player, and do they help others within the organization achieve their objectives?

Have a Proactive, Can-Do Attitude

What is the applicant's track record of accomplishing new things? When deciding to implement a new strategy, how did they go about assessing risk? Inquire about initiatives that the applicant has undertaken and that have failed. How did the applicant handle failure, and what did they learn from it?

People who have never failed have never accomplished what they are capable of, nor have they built the internal fortitude to recover from inevitable failures in the future.

There are people who see a world of possibilities and abundance versus those who see limitations and scarcity. You want to hire the former.

Possess the Skills to Do the Job or Can Rapidly Develop Them

It doesn't help your organization or the job candidate if there is a significant mismatch in know-how or credibility to do the job. If you want to place a high-potential individual into a stretch position, ensure they have the needed resources and advisors available to help them be successful.

Will Help You Become the Preferred Provider to Your Market

This is the Holy Grail of any business: To become the preferred provider of products or services in your geographic market, that is, the provider everyone wants to do business with.

To achieve preferred provider status, employees need to be focused on providing a great customer experience. This builds repeat business and is a real competitive strength.

Are People of Integrity

At some point in our careers, nearly all of us will find ourselves working with bosses, direct reports, or peers who lack ethics and integrity. These people are toxic and hinder the organization's ability to achieve its objectives.

Toxic people will throw others who stand in their way under the proverbial bus for their own purpose of advancing through the organization at the expense of others. They will complain about others and talk behind their backs to undermine them.

Those who are toxic are not trusted by their peers or direct reports. The actions of everyone they work with have a defensive component, which hinders any group from becoming a high-performance team. Toxic people within the organization don't realize that their personal integrity and reputation is a valuable asset. More on toxic people in Chapter 3-6.

Can Develop Other Leaders

Even if the job you are filling is that of an individual contributor and is not a formal leadership position, that individual should still have leadership potential. When serving on a team, an individual with the needed knowledge and expertise may need to step up and serve as the leader for a particular initiative.

Although this is advice to business leaders on the traits they should look for in new hires, the advice is also for those who want to improve their attractiveness to potential employers. For those seeking a new job, it will put you at a competitive advantage versus other applicants for any job for which you apply.

Hire Employees with Common Sense and Good Critical Judgment

Whenever I read in the news about an employee being terminated for violating a company policy by taking an action, either when that action avoids negative publicity or enhances the reputation of the company in the eyes of the public, I always ask myself, was the action of the employee the right thing to do? Sometimes the policy doesn't make sense, but it remains in effect and the employee is terminated anyway. This is not the signal you want to send to other employees and to the public.

There are good reasons for company policies and for holding employees accountable for following them. However, there are occasions when an employee should be celebrated rather than terminated for violating a company policy.

My Personal Experience

Many years ago, early in my career when I was national sales manager, one of our production plants reported that a product it had produced was found to have trace contaminants. We needed to recall the product that was shipped to a number of distributors, who in turn shipped the product to many end-users.

The cost of a recall increased significantly each day that passed. In addition, we faced a growing reputation and liability risk the longer the product remained in the marketplace. My boss, who was the division general manager, and the CEO were traveling and unreachable. This was before cell phones and e-mail. I did not have the authority to order the recall but waiting until they could be reached increased the cost and risk to the company. Therefore, I ordered the recall even though it was beyond my authority level to do so. When my boss and the CEO returned a number of days later, they thanked me for the decision I had made.

The lesson I learned as a young leader is to always hire people with common sense and good critical judgment. Someday, they may need to violate company policy or exceed their authority level in order to save the company money, reduce liability exposure, or protect its reputation. I also learned that as a leader, your reaction to an employee breaking company policy is situational. On occasion, disregarding policy is exactly what you want to happen, and the employee should be recognized for doing so.

Having good critical judgment means having the ability to weigh the consequences of an action that violates company policy. It means having the ability to determine whether the benefits of the action outweigh the possible negatives and be able to justify the action to your boss as having made the right decision. Having good critical judgment as a leader means having the ability to determine, in a particular situation, if your employee was justified in violating company policy.

Is violating company policy, even when it is in the best interest for the company to do so, a personal risk that might jeopardize your job? It depends on the company's leadership. The more political and performance capital you have, the more apt you will be celebrated than terminated.

Starbucks Philadelphia Incident

When making decisions, employees should exercise common sense and good critical judgment and fall back on the values, tone at the top, and organizational culture of the company. Employees should do the right thing to avoid negative publicity and damage to the company's reputation. At Starbucks, this did not occur during embarrassing incidents in Philadelphia and Tempe, Arizona.

In April 2018, two African American men, Donte Robinson and Rashon Nelson, didn't make a purchase within minutes after their arrival at a Starbucks in Rittenhouse Square neighborhood of Philadelphia. They told the café manager they were waiting for a friend to arrive. The café manager told the men to leave, and when they refused, the manager called the police and the two men were arrested.

Starbucks promotes its cafés as a comfortable and inviting place to meet friends, hang out, enjoy coffee, food, enjoy conversation with friends and use its Wi-Fi network. This is the business model that has made Starbucks successful. It is not unusual for people to arrive and not make a purchase as they wait for their friends.

Quoting from the Starbucks Values Statement,[12] "With our partners, our coffee and our customers at our core, we live these values ... creating a culture of warmth and belonging, where everyone is welcome." Perhaps not for everyone at this Starbucks that day.

To say that the arrest of these two individuals caused an uproar and accusations of bias and discrimination against black customers is an understatement. The incident went viral, and smartphone videos of the arrests were viewed around the world millions of times. There was a call to boycott Starbucks.

Immediately after the incident, Philadelphia police commissioner Richard Ross, who is African American, defended the actions of the police officers. However, a few days later, he changed his position and apologized to Robinson and Nelson.

In a public statement (NBC News), Ross said,[13]

[It] is apparently a well-known fact with Starbucks customers, but not everyone is aware that people spend long hours in Starbucks and aren't necessarily expected to make a purchase. ... It is also reasonable to believe that the officers [who responded to the 911 call] didn't know it either.

Starbucks apologized for the incident. A month later, Starbucks closed all of its 8,000 U.S.- based cafés for racial bias training.

---

[12] https://starbucks.com/about-us/company-information/mission-statement
[13] https://youtube.com/watch?v=zmYwF4IN5Gg

Starbucks Tempe Arizona Incident

During another embarrassing incident, on July 4, 2019, at a Starbucks in Tempe, Arizona, six police officers were asked to leave because a customer complained that she did not feel safe with the officers there.

An obligatory apology was made[14] by Rosann Williams, Starbucks executive vice president. Williams wrote to Tempe Chief of Police Sylvia Moir,

> On behalf of Starbucks, I want to sincerely apologize to you all for the experience that six of your officers had in our store on July 4. When those officers entered the store and a customer raised a concern over their presence, they should have been welcomed and treated with dignity and the upmost respect by our partners (employees). Instead, they were made to feel unwelcome and disrespected, which is completely unacceptable … We are already taking the necessary steps to ensure that this doesn't happen again.

Both the Philadelphia and Tempe Starbucks incidents sparked #BoycottStarbucks movements on social media. This is what can happen when an employee does not exercise common sense and good critical judgment.

> Lack of common sense and good critical judgment in employees is a risk factor that can damage a company's reputation. Hire people, especially those that deal with customers, with common sense and good critical judgment.

---

[14] https://stories.starbucks.com/press/2019/an-apology-to-the-tempe-police-department/

Whistleblower Hotlines: A Valuable Resource for Employees, CEOs, and Boards

Does your company have a whistleblower hotline in place? It should. Hotline reports from employees provide an opportunity for your company to address issues in a proactive manner and avoid or lessen financial liability and legal or reputational damage to your company.

Congress passed the Sarbanes-Oxley Act (SOX) in 2002, requiring public companies to put in place a whistleblower hotline to report fraud and illegal activity. Dodd-Frank legislation, passed by Congress in 2010, states that under certain circumstances, rewards be paid to whistleblowers who report securities violations and other illegal activities.

Hotlines were in use at some companies prior to SOX legislation, but they were not common. This legislation was passed in the wake of the 2001 accounting scandals at Enron, Tyco, WorldCom, and Adelphia Communications, resulting in criminal charges brought against the CEOs of those companies and the unprecedented dissolution of one of the "Big Five" accounting firms, Arthur Anderson, auditors of Enron. Many private companies as well as nonprofits now have a hotline in place.

Hotlines Are Important Due to Fear of Retaliation

In practice, employees use hotlines for anything they are uncomfortable reporting using normal company channels, mostly for fear of retaliation. In addition to fraud or illegal activities, these reports could run the gamut

from perceived violation of employee antidiscrimination laws, to violation of company travel and entertainment policies, to a tyrant in a management position making life miserable for direct reports.

The Audit Committee Ensures Hotline Complaints Are Investigated

The audit committee of the company's board often has the responsibility to review hotline reports and the results of the subsequent investigation. The hotline is monitored by the organization's internal auditor,
legal counsel, or in some cases, an outside firm. Whoever is monitoring
the hotline informs the chair of the audit committee and the CEO of
a hotline report, as long as the CEO is not the subject of the report, in
which case, the hotline monitor directly informs the chair of the audit
committee.

I have been a member of many board audit committees and chairman
of one. The CEOs of these organizations embrace the hotline as a valuable resource to uncover wrongdoing in their companies, and as a way
for corrective action to take place before an issue escalates out of control.
Boards view hotlines as a way to ensure they are made aware of issues that
require attention.

Are some hotline reports found to have little substance or are mali-
cious in some manner? Yes. All hotline reports, however, need to be investigated. That is part of the process. A rough measure of the climate within
an organization and a company's relationship with employees is reflected
in the types and substance of the hotline reports that are submitted.

Have there been instances in which whistleblowers using their company's hotline were retaliated against for reporting fraud or other illegal
actions? Yes. I discuss this in Chapter 4–10 titled, "Wells Fargo Scandal:
Failure in Leadership, Management, and Corporate Governance." Often
these situations become public, damaging the company's reputation. The
company runs the risk of being assessed huge monetary damages for retal-
iating against the employee. It takes courage for an employee to submit a
hotline report knowing that retaliation may occur. It goes without saying
that the manager who fires or orders the firing of an employee for using
the hotline must be fired.

In an October 25, 2014 article in the *Harvard Law School Forum on Corporate Governance and Financial Regulation*,[15] Kobi Kastiel wrote,

SEC Chair Mary Jo White recently commented that it is up to company directors, along with senior management under the purview of the board, to set the all-important "tone at the top" for the entire company. *Setting the standard in the boardroom that good corporate governance and rigorous compliance are essential helps establish a strong corporate culture throughout a company.*

Recognition by employees throughout the organization that hotline reports are taken seriously, are visible to members of the board, and are effectively investigated and resolved sends a very strong message about the high standards to which all employees will be held regarding ethics and obeying the law.

Employees pick up on everything, including the tone set by the organization's leadership. CEOs, set the right values, standards of ethical behavior, and the right tone within your company. Ensure all employees are informed about the existence of the hotline and ensure that those submitting hotline reports learn of the results of the investigation. You will significantly reduce the possibility of a scandal and damage to the reputation of your organization.

---

[15] https://corpgov.law.harvard.edu/2014/10/25/elements-of-an-effective-whistleblower-hotline/

Assessing Employee Performance and Sharing Feedback

Figure 1-14 Don't run the risk of losing a high-performing employee.

Photo: Warchi Collecton/Getty Images

As CEO, have you ever been concerned about the effectiveness of your company's leaders in assessing the performance of their employees? Do you know if your employees are satisfied with your organization's performance management and compensation systems?

Common Complaints from Employees

I have heard many comments from employees that they rarely get feedback from their boss about how they are performing. Many employees are never told how base salaries and salary increases are determined or what the midpoint is of their position. There is no reason not to be transparent.

When an employee would tell me that they were not happy with what they were paid, I told them that they were compensated competitively based on market survey data and their performance. If they wanted to earn more, they had to improve their performance or get promoted to a higher paying job.

Some employees feel that there are insufficient salary dollars allocated to bring top performers to a salary level reflective of their performance and contributions to the company. *A company should never underpay a high-performing employee. It's one of the reasons they leave. Not only does the company run the risk of losing the employee, they may go to work for a competitor.*

When I was president of PQ's Canadian subsidiary, our top technical expert on the pulp and paper industry submitted his resignation to go with one of our customers. I told him he didn't have permission to leave and worked out with him what it would take for him to stay with our company. He stayed, received an increase in compensation and responsibility, and continued to advance the state-of-the-art use of our products to that industry. The lesson—always keep your high-performing employees.

Treat Employees Fairly

I recently received an e-mail from a former employee who reminded me of the principle of pay equity in the workplace. She wrote:

> I will always remember our lunch where you spoke to me about fairness and leadership. … You adjusted my pay by 27%. You said it was a travesty that I was not paid as much as my fellow male workers and that you were going to right the wrong. This episode still remains with me over 30 years later. Your leadership and insight taught me that whatever the situation, honesty and fairness will always win out.

I adjusted her compensation because it was the right thing to do.

Assessing Performance

A major responsibility of every boss is to assess the performance of those individuals who report to them and provide feedback on strengths and areas for improvement. Feedback should be periodic during the year, thanking the employee for a job well done, and offering coaching when improvement is needed.

Once a year, a more formal assessment is helpful to both the boss and the employee. I have always asked my direct reports to write their own report on their performance versus goals and then compare it to my own assessment when we meet to review their performance. This is a valuable way to get dialogue going between the boss and the employee.

Write the performance assessments in prose, which is more effective than just "checking boxes" that describe levels of performance. Inform employees whether they are meeting expectations and coach them on how to improve their performance. Do this periodically throughout the year. You should part company with employees who continually fall short of expectations and do not improve over time.

360-Degree Feedback

A 360-degree anonymous feedback process can provide a more complete picture of an employee's leadership style and behaviors. Data is collected from the employee's direct reports and peers to get a sense of how well the employee works with others in the organization.

Some people feel that the results of the 360-degree feedback process should only be shared with the employee as a developmental tool. I disagree. The boss should also receive the report to understand how the employee is interacting with their direct reports and their peers.

Be sure to provide performance feedback periodically to your employees. There is no reason why your company's performance management and compensation system should not be transparent and easily understood by everyone. It will remove any doubts that they are not being treated in a fair and equitable manner. This allows employees to focus on their job and not compensation issues. It will also help to retain top performers. Companies where this occurs will perform better over the long run.

Within some organizations, employees are fearful of providing candid 360-degree feedback about their boss due to concerns they will rain down retribution on those they think may have provided negative feedback. This is an indictment of the organizational culture, as well as the CEO and the board for allowing this culture to exist.

> If the employees in your company have concerns about your com-
> pany's performance management system, listen to their concerns
> and address them. If some employees are reluctant to provide can-
> did 360-degree input about their boss due to fear of retribution,
> you need to part company with that boss as soon as possible.

CHAPTER 1-15

Do You Have a Tyrant Reporting to You?

Tyrants who disrespect their direct reports cause untold damage to the performance of their organization as well as make life miserable for those who work for them. These managers tend to micromanage, blame others for their mistakes, and sap the creativity, initiative, and vitality from the workplace. They also adversely impact the ability of people to make decisions without "checking with the boss."

Bad Managers Drive Out Good Employees

No one can effectively do their job in an atmosphere of fear and intimidation. No employee should have to work in such a toxic environment. The best people don't put up with it, and they eventually leave the company, resulting in a significant loss of talent that will adversely impact the firm's performance and potential for growth.

Effective leaders don't criticize their employees in public. It shows lack of emotional intelligence. Leaders that do this drive out good employees. It should not be tolerated by the CEO, and if the individual is the CEO, not tolerated by the board of directors.

My personal experience working for a tyrant is described in Chapter 3–6. It was prior to the introduction of whistleblower hotlines. The human resources department did not have a strong leader, and I did not want to risk going to executive management, so there was no path to lodge a complaint. I was very close to leaving the company. Had I left, the company would have been deprived of a future CEO.

I was promoted to be the tyrant's peer and then promoted to be his boss. He continued to create an atmosphere of fear and intimidation, so I fired him.

I replaced the tyrant with a very effective leader. It took him months to bring the division's employees to the point where they were again operating as they should. Once more, they were making decisions on their own. They were exercising initiative and creativity, taking personal ownership of their part of the business and not being fearful of making a mistake, which was career threatening under the former manager.

Many tyrants "manage up" very well. As a leader, it is your responsibility to see through this and ensure that their direct reports are treating their people professionally and with respect.

Employees Need to Trust the Hotline

It is important to ensure that there is no retaliation against any employee who uses the whistleblower hotline to report a tyrant. If the company's employees do not have confidence in the leadership of the company, they may be fearful of using the hotline. If this is the case, the company has issues beyond the tyrant.

What should you do if one of your direct reports is a tyrant? Don't tolerate it. If the individual doesn't rapidly change, you need to part company with them.

Staff Unit Leaders: Don't Adopt Policies That Micromanage Line Operating or Other Staff Units

Have you ever worked in an organization where policies that were put in place by overzealous staff groups went beyond what is necessary to ensure uniform practices across the organization and compliance with legal or regulatory requirements?

Do Some Policies Have No Discernible Benefit?

Effective leaders ask if some of their firm's policies are unnecessary, because they have no discernible benefit or have outlived their usefulness. Do some policies or practices micromanage decisions that should be within a line or staff unit leader's discretion? Are some policies unnecessarily restrictive and impede the ability of line or staff unit leaders to do their jobs?

Policies attract internal auditing resources to ensure compliance. Auditing policies which are unnecessary divert resources away from important compliance or other areas. They also may impede the freedom of leaders of line and staff units from taking action or making decisions. Don't write policies and procedures unless they are necessary to adhere to a core value or compliance requirement, or ensure consistent practice across the company, such as with human resource policies.

Should policies and practices that make little sense or impede the success of a staff or line unit be challenged? Absolutely! It is surprising how often this does not occur. Many employees feel "that's just the way it is." Not true. Policies and practices that don't make sense need to be challenged and changed.

Don't Adopt Across-the-Board Policies Due to the Transgressions of a Few

How many of us have worked in an organization where, due to the lack of common sense and good critical judgment of a few, blanket policies are adopted for the entire organization? *These few employees should be dealt with on an individual basis. Across the board policies could hamper those employees with common sense and good critical judgment from doing their jobs.*

Don't micromanage leaders. Empower them and hold them accountable for results. Don't adopt across the board policies due to the transgressions of a few.

When Asked About Changing a Policy That Doesn't Make Sense, Don't Respond "Well, That's Just the Way It Is"

Most of us have run into policies at work that don't seem to make any sense. They impede the ability of the company to implement change and achieve its goals. Without the influence or authority to change them, employees are frustrated, wondering why these policies remain in place.

Every company needs policies and procedures to effectively serve its customers or clients, ensure equitable treatment of employees, protect against litigation, and adhere to legal and regulatory requirements. Without them, there would be chaos.

Policies That Don't Make Sense Should Be Challenged

At the first anniversary of my job as a process engineer at PQ Corporation, I received a performance review and was told that I was being awarded a salary increase of five percent, compared with a marketplace salary structure increase of four percent. During our conversation, my boss made the mistake of telling me that the other engineer in our small group would be awarded an increase of three percent.

I thought my co-worker was a solid performer and questioned why his salary increase was less than the marketplace increase. My boss said that the overall percentage salary increase for our small department could not exceed the increase in the salary structure—four percent. I told him that made no sense. My boss responded, "Well, that's just the way it is."

I then told my boss that when I rose to a level within the company where I could influence or change the system, I would. That compensation system didn't fulfill what I thought should be its intended objective, which is to pay employees commensurate with their performance.

Years later, I was appointed to the position of president of PQ's global Industrial Chemicals Group. I now had the influence to change the compensation system, which over the years had undergone minor changes, but could be more effective.

I convinced the other two operating group presidents, the resistant leader of the human resources department and PQ's CEO, of the need to change how we compensated our employees.

The new performance and compensation system that was developed had input from employee focus groups, which created buy-in. The employees liked it because it provided a more rational approach to compensation administration. Employees also had ownership in the system, since a group of them helped develop it.

Achieve the Right Balance Between Time Spent on Bureaucracy and Time Spent on Achieving Results

How many of us have worked in bureaucratic organizations in which overly prescriptive policies, procedures, and controls approach the point where employees are micromanaged and encroach on time better spent running and growing the business and providing a great customer or client experience? Unfortunately, too many of us.

Each year we wrote detailed business plans. These documents outlined not only the objectives of the business, but also the detailed strategies to accomplish them. Due to changes in the business environment, many business plans became obsolete after they were written. Perhaps that's why they often just sat in a desk drawer or in a bookcase in someone's office until a year passed and it was time to write the next business plan, while time was spent adjusting the strategy in real time.

Many of us are required to write lengthy reports, communicating to our bosses our activities and results accomplished during the month or quarter. Shouldn't we only be focusing on communicating what's important? Is there a better way of informing upper management of this information?

Business plans and monthly/quarterly progress reports serve a purpose. The question is: How can that purpose be most effectively served with the least amount of bureaucracy, and without taking a leader's time away from operating the business? What is the right balance?

To address the issue of burdensome bureaucracy in my company, when I became CEO, I reduced written detailed reports sent to me to the minimum and focused on what was important. Written reports consisted of a one or two-page executive summary. The amount of verbal reporting was significantly increased. This had the benefit of increasing the dialogue between me and my direct reports, and made for better decision making and understanding of the issues facing the business. It also created more time to operate and grow the business.

Challenging policies and procedures is a good thing. Some policies address issues that no longer exist, and now only increase bureaucracy and hamper the operation of the business. When policies no longer serve a useful purpose, they need to go.

CEOs, listen to those employees who challenge policies that don't make sense to them. Never respond with, "Well, that's just the way it is." These employees are your talented change agents. If frustration leads them to leave your company, they may go to work for a competitor.

Not Getting What You Need from a Corporate Staff Unit?

As I came up through the ranks of PQ Corporation, a company with multiple business units operating in 19 countries, the issue of the support that business units receive from corporate staff units was always a subject of discussion. The saying, "I am from corporate and I am here to help you," and the occasional negative reaction from business units are familiar to many.

The most frequent complaints from business units about corporate staff units are I am not getting the support I need; the support I am getting is not worth what I am being charged; and I can buy the same service cheaper on the outside. These complaints will always be a subject of discussion.

Companies in multiple lines of business are organized by business units, in which the general manager of each business unit reports up through a hierarchy to the CEO. These general managers are held accountable for the bottom-line results of the P&L statement of their respective businesses. Business units receive services from corporate staff units, which also report up to the CEO, but through a different hierarchy.

At smaller companies, often there are no business units or general managers who have responsibility for P&L statements. Functional line operating departments and staff units all report up through their respective hierarchies to the CEO, who has responsibility for the P&L statement of the entire company.

Business units are the internal customers of corporate staff units. Occasionally, some staff units don't realize this and don't give the business units the support they need. Staff units should be doing everything they can to be responsive to the needs of the business units. Business units and staff units must partner and collaborate to achieve success of the business units and the company as a whole.

A critical issue arises when a business unit is not getting what it needs from a staff unit to drive its growth, bottom-line results, or strategic initiatives. Business units can always add the needed resources from outside the company and pay for it themselves if funds within the business unit are available.

If you are the general manager of a business unit, you are held accountable for your business unit's bottom line. Because of this P&L responsibility, if you can't get what you need from a corporate staff unit to help you meet your bottom-line goals, you need to have a conversation with the leader of that staff unit. If that doesn't work, take the issue to your boss and if necessary, eventually to the CEO of the company.

I would not be bashful in taking this issue up the organization for resolution. Just do it in a politically sensitive way. Your goals are one element of the CEO's goals, and the CEO is evaluated by the board on the results of the entire company. The CEO will want to help you get what you need to achieve your goals.

Set Realistic Goals to Drive Earnings Growth

Figure 1-19 Establish a goal-setting approach that balances upside potentials with down side risks.

Photo: Daizuoxin Collection/Getty Images

One of the most important decisions of any leader is to set annual financial goals for their organization. Should they set realistic goals, or tough stretch goals with a lower probability of achievement?

Shark Tank Star Kevin O'Leary's Experience

At the 2018 Disruptor 50 conference in Philadelphia, Shark Tank star Kevin O'Leary discussed the factors that influenced the return of capital of the 37 companies within his venture portfolio. O'Leary said, "A study showed ... 90 percent of the [cash] returns came from companies run by women." Why? O'Leary said,

Companies run by men hit their quarterly sales targets 65 percent of the time. … Women-led companies hit their targets 95 percent of the time. … If you are on a winning team in any sport … you have a winning culture. Winning cultures have different metrics than just financial reward. Being part of a winning team is powerful. These [women-led] teams are constantly hitting their targets.

O'Leary talks about his views in a March 2018 *CNBC* article headlined, "Shark Tank Star Kevin O'Leary: Women-Run Businesses Make Me the Most Money. Here's Why."[16] In this article, O'Leary said,

If employees aren't meeting their goals, … frustration can lead to turnover, which is particularly costly for small operations. Women are better at avoiding this pitfall. When you meet your goals 95 percent of the time, you change the culture of your business. People feel they're working in a winning organization. … That's why women are doing better in business—they keep their people. The staff are sticky. They want to work there because they're hitting their goals. … You don't have to reach for the stars, you want to win 95 percent of the time. That's the secret sauce.

My Own Goal-Setting Experience Was Similar to Kevin O'Leary's

As a mid-level leader at my company, I lived through many years of CEOs setting what nearly everyone on the leadership team felt was an unrealistically high annual corporate earnings goal. When we started to lag behind the goal, costs were cut in a losing effort to try to close the performance gap between the actual result and the goal. This was a debilitating exercise that took its toll on morale. Who were we kidding?

When setting goals, we found that people were optimistic and often overstate upside potentials and understate downside risks. This contributed to missing the goal.

---

[16] https://cnbc.com/2018/03/22/shark-tanks-kevin-oleary-women-make-me-the-most-money.html

After I was named CEO of PQ, I changed our annual financial goal-setting approach. We were much more realistic in balancing the upside potential with the downside risk of possible adverse market events. Each business unit set goals that were reasonably attainable, based on strategies that provided a path toward achievement. However, I set the expectation that financial goals were only a waypoint that should be exceeded by the greatest extent possible, and our employees should have fun doing so.

The morale changed significantly within the company. Instead of a debilitating atmosphere in which we lagged our earnings goal during the year, employees took satisfaction in tracking above goal each month and quarter. The better the financial performance, the higher the bonus payment for that portion of the bonus tied to financial results. We were completely transparent by sharing with the employees the bonus pool formula, and they were energized as their results increased the size of the pool as well as their own possible bonus opportunity.

Our employee incentive program was not driven by achieving the earnings goal, but by achieving earnings growth as a calculated percentage above the three previous years' earnings results, based upon what was appropriate for our industry. The higher the actual earnings achieved, the higher the bonuses, and the higher the profit-sharing pool in which all employees participated.

The shareholders of the company don't know what the annual earnings goal for the company is and don't care. They only care about year-over-year earnings growth and if the investment returns exceed those of similar companies within the industry.

PQ business unit leaders occasionally wanted to build a reserve (i.e., commit to a lower earnings number) in their goals, if there were downside risks in their business plans not offset by upside potentials. I permitted them to do so. Adding up all the earnings of the business units, I would consider whether the corporate earnings goal was reasonably attainable. If not, I would build a president's reserve into the company's earnings goal.

As the months passed, employees developed and executed strategies to exceed their goals. With this approach, PQ's earnings grew from $14 million (adjusted for an adverse material competitive situation) to $43 million over the five years that included 9/11 and the severe recession of 2002. This compared with flat earnings during the previous three years.

After 2000, we never had a down quarter. As measured by revenue growth, earnings growth, and return on assets, we moved from fourth quartile performance to first quartile performance, compared with 17 public peer companies within the chemical industry.

I did not achieve these earnings results—the men and women who operated our businesses around the world achieved them. I focused on tone at the top, corporate culture, ensuring we have the right people in senior leadership positions, and on corporate strategy. I didn't use O'Leary's phrases, "winning team" and "winning culture," to describe what we created. But thinking back, those are the phrases to describe the change in the organization at that time.

The goal-setting process is a means to an end—great performance. Financial goals should only be an intermediate target, and exceeded by the greatest extent possible, in an upbeat environment where employees are rewarded handsomely for their performance.

Sometimes, Bad Things Happen, Regardless of Your Tone at the Top

Regardless of a leader's tone at the top and the culture they nurture within their organization, bad things can occur that run counter to the values espoused by that leader.

My Own Experience

While I was CEO of PQ Corporation, during a heavy rainstorm, one of our plant managers discharged highly alkaline process water down a sewer to protect electrical equipment from damage due to rising rainwater levels. The plant didn't have a permit to discharge the process water.

The Environmental Protection Agency (EPA) noticed a spike in the pH of water in the sewer and traced the source back to our plant. When questioned by the EPA if the source of the high pH water was his plant, the plant manager said no. Had he told the truth, the plant would have most likely received a modest fine and warned not to have the incident re-occur.

However, because the plant manager was not truthful when he responded to the EPA's question, the company was charged with a violation of the Federal Clean Water Act and subjected to harsh financial penalties. PQ's environmental performance was then investigated by the EPA, which found that we were in compliance with environmental laws at all of our other plants.

The plant manager was terminated, and the board launched an investigation into my tone at the top and the culture within the organization, to determine if I was indirectly complicit in the plant manager's actions. If the board found that the tone I set and the culture I nurtured as the CEO did not make it clear to all employees that they were to act ethically and obey local, state, and federal laws, I could have been terminated.

Fortunately, my actions, remarks, and written communications to employees over time demonstrated that I espoused a very strong ethical tone and culture. However, as CEO of the company, the illegal act by the plant manager occurred on my watch. The board sanctioned me by significantly reducing my bonus that year, which was the right thing to do. What protected me from termination was tangible proof of my strong tone at the top and the organizational culture that I nurtured.

Leaders, the reputation of your company and your personal reputation depends on the tone and culture that you espouse and how you respond after an unethical act occurs. Ensure that the people throughout all levels of your organization know your values and your expectations of them.

Audit mission-critical areas to ensure rules are being followed and innocent errors are caught. These audits must be performed centrally, and not within business units. When bad things do occur, you want the incident to be viewed as an aberrant violation of your values and not a reflection of your tone at the top and the culture that you have nurtured.

CHAPTER 1-21

Do Your Employees See Your HR Department as a Friend or Foe?

The reputation of the Human Resource department at some organizations has been damaged due to their reaction/inaction to employee-reported incidents of wrongdoing. This undermines the trust that employees should have in HR, the company's CEO, and its board of directors.

Roles of the HR Department

One of the many roles of HR is to protect employees from wrongdoing by their boss or other employees. Another role is to help defend the organization from employee lawsuits. Is HR a friend or foe of employees?

The tone at the top and corporate culture that governs an organization's behavior are both set by the CEO and driven by HR and all the leaders within the company. It is up to the board of directors to hold the CEO accountable for tone, culture, values, and ethics. If the board fails in these responsibilities, the reputation of the organization is threatened.

The Lesson Taught by Uber

Under former CEO Travis Kalanick, Uber's reputation was damaged when engineer Susan[17] Fowler went public in a blog she wrote on February 19, 2017, accusing the company of tolerating a culture of sexual harassment. Fowler described the lack of support by HR that she and many other women experienced when they reported sexual harassment

[17] https://susanjfowler.com/blog/2017/2/19/reflecting-on-one-very-strange-year-at-uber

by their bosses. Many women decided to leave the company rather than work in a toxic environment.

No organization can afford to develop a reputation where female employees are not respected. Due to this and other accusations of wrong-doing, it was two major investors,[18] not the Uber board, who told Kalanick he needed to step down from the position of CEO. Why didn't the Uber board remove Kalanick themselves?

The Lesson Taught by Wells Fargo

Wells Fargo's reputation was seriously damaged due to the scandal that rocked the bank during the fourth quarter of 2016 when it became public that, since 2011, employees within the retail banking business created as many as 3.5 million fraudulent accounts to meet management-imposed sales quotas of the bank's incentive compensation program.

Establishing fraudulent accounts is bad enough. In a September 21, 2016 *CNN Money* article,[19] Matt Egan wrote that a number of Wells Fargo employees were fired for reporting unethical practices to HR and the bank's ethics hotline.

Quoting Eagan's article,

One former Wells Fargo human resources official even said the bank had a method in place to retaliate against tipsters. He said that Wells Fargo would find ways to fire employees "in retaliation for shining light" on sales issues. It could be as simple as monitoring the employee to find a fault, like showing up a few minutes late on several occasions.

Perhaps these employees didn't report their concerns to HR because they didn't trust them, and as it turns out, for good reason. More on Wells Fargo in Chapter 4–10.

---

[18] https://nytimes.com/2017/06/21/technology/uber-travis-kalanick-final-hours.html

[19] https://money.cnn.com/2016/09/21/investing/wells-fargo-fired-workers-retaliation-fake-accounts/

It is a common board governance practice for hotline reports to go to the audit committee of the board. Whenever the committee receives a hotline report of wrongdoing, management or an outside law firm is charged with investigating it. It goes without saying that the hotline reporter must not face retaliation.

Human Resources can serve an important role by being a listener, counselor, and problem solver when issues with a boss arise, if HR is trusted by the employees. By serving as a sounding board for employee complaints, they often defuse concerns and prevent them from becoming major issues. Ensure HR plays this role.

PART 2

Building Competitive Advantage

CHAPTER 2-1

Understand Your Competitive Position

Figure 2-1 Develop a SWOT analysis for your business, identifying strengths, weaknesses, opportunities and threats.

Photo: Audrey Popov/Getty Images

Before you develop strategies to build competitive advantage, you need to understand your company's competitive position in the marketplace. Michael Porter, professor at the Harvard Business School, once said, "Strategy is about setting yourself apart from the competition. It's not a matter of being better at what you do—it's a matter of being different at what you do."[20]

A company's ability to set itself apart from competition is in part based on its position within the industries in which it participates. In his book,

---

[20] https://azquotes.com/quote/871412

Competitive Strategy: Techniques for Analyzing Industries and Competitors, Porter identifies five forces that impact the competitiveness of a company:

1. Number of competitors within an industry
   Are there many companies against which to compete, increasing the importance of differentiating your company from your competitors?
2. Ease of entry of a new competitor
   Is entry of a new competitor difficult due to the capital intensiveness of the business or the difficulty of gaining access to state-of-the-art technology?
3. Supplier concentration
   Are there few suppliers in the industry, which gives them power to dictate the price and terms under which they sell products or services?
4. Customer concentration
   Are there few large customers, which gives them power to dictate the price and terms under which they buy products or services?
5. Threat from substitutes
   How easy is it for a customer or client to use a substitute product or service?

If a company is in multiple businesses, these five forces may be different for each business. In addition to understanding these five forces, business leaders should prepare a SWOT analysis for each of their businesses, understanding their strengths, weaknesses, opportunities, and threats. *Strategies can then be developed to build on strengths, address weaknesses, take advantage of opportunities, and defend against threats.* To the extent the information is available, develop a SWOT analysis of your competitors .

The following chapters in this section share guidance on strategies to build competitive advantage to achieve the Holy Grail of any business—to become the preferred provider of products or services to its marketplace.

Become the Preferred Provider to Your Markets— The Holy Grail of Any Business

There is one universal principle that determines the degree of success of all businesses: Be the preferred provider to your markets.

What Is a "Preferred Provider"?

It's a provider that a customer or client favors in the purchase of a product or service versus its competition. A preferred provider has a significant competitive advantage over all other providers, because it is the "go-to" provider in the marketplace. Whether a business sells autos, groceries, clothing, computers, bicycles, or raw materials to a manufacturer of industrial products, it wants to be the preferred provider of those products.

Whether a business is an Internet service provider, a hospital, or a physician, an attorney, accountant, or a roofing company, it wants to be the preferred provider of those services.

So, how does a business build competitive advantage by becoming the preferred provider to the markets it serves? It differentiates itself from competitors by excelling in the following areas.

Offers High-Quality, Reliable Products and Services

When customers buy a product, they expect that it meets a high standard of quality and it will work as intended. They don't want to waste time and effort returning a shoddy product to have it replaced. When clients buy a service, they expect that service to be performed in a professional and competent manner.

People will return to buy products and services from those companies that always meet their commitments. Companies earn repeat business when the price charged is fair for the value received, and when they make it easy for a consumer to interact with them. Customer service representatives that only go through the motions without taking a genuine interest in helping a customer drive repeat business away and hurts the company's reputation.

Provides a Great Customer Experience

I have been biking for over 20 years, and my preferred provider of bikes, equipment, and repair services is AAAA Bike Shop in Ventnor, NJ. The proprietors are Mike and Ann Marie Wiesen, who go out of their way to provide a great customer experience.

When I purchased my road bike from Wiesen six years ago, he asked me what type of bike I currently rode. I told him I rode a hybrid bike but wanted to switch to a road bike. Wiesen asked me whether I was a leisurely or a serious biker, the distance I usually rode, and the type of handlebar configuration I would be most comfortable with—drop down or flat. He lent me two bikes to try out. After making my choice and choosing the right bike height, Wiesen ordered it for me.

I have been back to AAAA Bike Shop many times for normal maintenance, which is always prompt and done right the first time. I have subsequently purchased three bikes for my grandkids from the shop. The Wiesens certainly differentiate their bike shop versus their competition with personalized service.

Delights the Customer

I recently received a phone call from a friend whose kitchen skylight broke just hours before it was forecasted to rain and didn't know who to call for a temporary repair. I called Chuck Goss, the president of Cooper Roofing Inc. for whom I had done consulting work the previous year. Within an hour, a Cooper crew arrived at her home and covered the skylight opening with plywood just before it started to rain. A few days later, Cooper replaced the skylight.

My friend was delighted by how quickly and professionally Cooper Roofing responded to her problem. Don't you think that she will be singing the praises of Cooper Roofing to all of her friends?

Is Trustworthy

Customers want to do business with a company that will act in the customer's best interest. When a company acts in this manner, it earns the customers' trust. When a company acts in its own best interest and against the interests of its customers, it earns its customers' wrath.

Is on a Journey To Be the Best in the World at What It Does

Why should you be on this journey? Because it builds competitive advantage and makes it more difficult for other companies to compete with you. This also focuses employees on what builds great, enduring companies.

Many companies will be on the journey to be the preferred provider. The company that does it best, wins.

So, what is one of the prime cultural norms of companies on a journey to become the preferred provider to its market? Their employees have a shared purpose, which is to ensure that those who buy from them have a great customer/client experience. Your goal is to be so good at being the preferred provider that your competitors think it's very difficult to compete against you.

CHAPTER 2-3

Provide a Great Customer Experience

How often does our experience as a customer, client, or spectator at an event fall short of our expectations? The first rule of any provider of a product, service, or experience is to think like a customer, client, or spectator and ask, "What would be my expectations, and how would I like to see my expectations met, and then exceeded? How would I like to be personally treated?"

Operationalize the Customer Experience

As a provider, how do you ensure that you will exceed your customer's, client's or spectator's expectations? You should "operationalize" their experience. You should think through every encounter and interaction in detail and determine whether they would have a great experience dealing with your organization. Is it easy for a customer, client, or guest to speak with the right person to have their problem resolved? Are they treated in a courteous manner? Does your company always meet its commitments?

In a May 2018 *Entrepreneur.com* article by Katie Lundin headlined "Five reasons why your business is losing customers,"[21] she listed the following reasons: "You're guilty of poor customer experience, your product or service failed to meet expectations, you didn't show value, your business is inconsistent, and your sales tactics are out-of-date." These are commonsense things businesses should not do. Focus on these areas, and you will gain competitive advantage over those companies that don't.

---

[21] https://entrepreneur.com/article/313463

The Pope's Visit to Philadelphia

In September 2015, during Pope Francis's visit to Philadelphia, the expectations of many attendees with tickets to the papal mass were not met. Many were not able to enter the Parkway security zone in time to see Pope Francis and participate in the mass due to an insufficient number of security check points. Some check points were prematurely closed for no apparent reason before the crowds could be cleared to enter the security zone, and they were shuffled to other check points that were overcrowded. Some visitors who traveled great distances to participate in the Pope's mass couldn't get into the Parkway area.

The Ben Franklin Bridge, a major thoroughfare connecting Camden, New Jersey, and Philadelphia, was closed to vehicle traffic, but was open to pedestrians. From the New Jersey side of the bridge to the Parkway where the Pope celebrated mass, the walk was over 3 miles each way, a nearly impossible trek by the elderly wanting to see the Pope.

Why wasn't bus service offered across the bridge and to a security entrance at the Parkway? New Jersey Transportation Commissioner Jamie Fox stated, "If you are not prepared to walk a considerable distance, you may want to reconsider your attendance." Apparently, his mindset was not to deliver a great visitor experience.

It should be noted that the Transportation Safety Administration (TSA) was responsible for security, not the City of Philadelphia. The TSA should have operationalized the security screening process and ensured there were a sufficient number of check points. They did not view the security screening process through the eyes of the papal mass attendees.

The TSA had much less at stake in providing a great visitor experience than the city's administration, whose goal should have been for visitors to feel like welcomed guests and enjoy their stay in Philadelphia. That goal should have been for visitors to depart with the belief that Philadelphia ranks with the preeminent cities of the world, which over the long term attracts more visitors, businesses, and residents to the city. They could have done a better job achieving this goal.

Leaders, operationalize interactions with your customers, clients, or guests. View the customer experience through their eyes. Make adjustments to how you execute to ensure they have a great experience interacting with your organization. Treat your clients, customers, and guests as you would like to be treated. Meet and then exceed their expectations. Build competitive advantage.

CHAPTER 2-4

Treat Customers Like You Would Like To Be Treated

Not long ago, I had a great customer experience at the Apple store on Walnut Street in Philadelphia—one that I would rate as the gold standard for any business that wants to create a competitive advantage.

I had purchased an iPhone for my wife online and wanted to buy her a protective case for her new phone. When I entered the store, I was greeted by Apple specialist Carol Rabuck, who after personally showing me available phone case choices, asked if I would be interested in trying Apple Pay to purchase the case. She set up my own iPhone to do so.

After Rabuck showed me how to enable a number of features on my iPhone, I left the store with a feeling that Rabuck treated me like she would like to be treated.

The leadership at Apple recognizes that their products and service are customer service intensive. In addition to being in the core business of providing personal computers and mobile communication devices, Apple is also in the core business of providing a great customer experience. Their goal is preeminence. They get it right. Other companies in customer service–intensive businesses do not.

The leaders at many companies have yet to recognize that providing a great customer experience is a significant competitive differentiator. A company is known by the customer experience it delivers. When a company doesn't deliver a great customer experience, its reputation suffers.

A friend of mine had been in an auto accident and had a very difficult customer experience getting his health care insurance provider to pay medical expenses above the amount covered by his auto insurance provider. His credit rating was adversely affected because these medical bills had not been paid.

After spending significant time on the phone with numerous call center employees of his health care insurance provider, he was finally told that they needed documentation to prove that his auto insurance provider had paid medical expenses up to his policy limit.

A proactive healthcare insurance provider that treats policy holders as valued clients would have a corporate culture and system in place to ensure that their policy holder's medical expenses are promptly paid so their credit rating is not harmed. By not having this proactive culture in place, the health insurance provider sends a signal to the client that he is not valued.

This is not how the executives at the health insurance company would like to be personally treated.

Why don't the leaders at all businesses strive to treat customers and clients like they would like to be treated? Those that do will find it to be a significant competitive differentiator.

CHAPTER 2-5

In Business, Good Is the Enemy of Great

"Good is the enemy of great" are the opening words of *Good to Great*, the best-selling iconic book by preeminent leadership and management thought leader Jim Collins, on "why some companies make the leap [to outstanding sustained performance] … and some don't."

If You Think that "Good" Is Good Enough, You Will Never Become Great

When I became the president and CEO of PQ Corporation, chairman of the PQ board Richard D. Wood Jr. gave me a copy of *Good to Great*. I will be forever grateful to Wood, because Collins' book served as a guide for leading PQ during my tenure as CEO, and later serving as an independent board member at other companies.

Collins and his team of researchers poured over reams of data to uncover 11 companies that had cumulative stock returns at least 6.9 times that of the general market over a 15-year period.

Collins and his team then studied the characteristics of these companies and the characteristics of their CEOs, versus comparison companies that did not perform as well. Collins identified eight principles that differentiated high-performing companies from the comparison companies. Here are the four differentiating principles that were most impactful to me.

Surround Yourself with the Right People

Get the "right people on the bus [and] the right people in the right seats … [and they will] figure out how to take it someplace great." Collins states that leaders should start with "who," not "where," since the right people will decide the strategic direction of the enterprise and when a change in direction is needed, they will decide what that change should be. By having the right people decide the strategic direction and goals for the organization, they own them, and they will be more committed to achieving them.

Level 5 Leaders Build Enduring Greatness

Collins identifies a Level 5 leader as one who "builds enduring greatness through a paradoxical blend of personal humility and professional will." Collins goes on to state that Level 5 leaders are very ambitious, but "their ambition is first and foremost for the institution, not themselves."

Level 5 leaders are not imperial leaders. They do not self-aggrandize and are not focused on the perks of their position. To the contrary, they are focused on building teams within the company that can achieve great results, led by effective leaders throughout the organization who can inspire their people. Level 5 leaders have an iron will to be successful, and they inspire their employees to greatness. Observing many CEOs over time, my experience is that Level 5 CEOs are more successful in the long run than imperial CEOs.

Achieving Greatness Is a Journey, One That Never Ends

Once you think you are great, you have nowhere to go but down. Very few organizations ever achieve greatness, even though at times leaders and those who they lead may use that term to describe their organizations. As CEO of PQ, I would tell our employees never to refer to our company as great. This is for third parties to do, and our response should always be, "Thank you, but we are on a journey, and have a long way to go to achieve greatness."

Regardless of your position in a company, always remember you are on a journey that never ends, and that good is the enemy of great.

Andy Grove Was Right. Only the Paranoid Survive

Andy Grove, former chairman and CEO of Intel Corp., coined the phrase, "Only the paranoid survive." Grove has given us a timeless lesson on the need for a company to be paranoid about staying ahead of the competition and anticipating market trends. Many companies don't realize that there may be a current or new competitor out there targeting their customers or that markets change over time.

The Pennsylvania Railroad, Kodak, and the Taxicab Industry Didn't Recognize Market and Technology Trends Until It Was Too Late

One only needs to consider the mighty Pennsylvania Railroad (PRR), which after World War Two faced increasing competition from air and auto travel and by the construction of the Interstate Highway system. PRR saw themselves in the railroad business, not the business of transporting passengers and freight, which today, for freight, is very lucrative.

Kodak missed the transformation to digital photo technology in their industry, because they viewed themselves as being in the film business, not the business of capturing images. They ceded their dominance in the photo industry to digital technology. There are many other examples of companies not being paranoid about their business.

Uber saw an opportunity to provide the traditional taxicab market with an on-demand car service that leverages a device nearly all of us carry—an iPhone or Android smartphone. Founded in 2009, Uber developed a mobile app for requesting and paying for car services through the convenience of a smartphone.

To state that Uber has been widely successful is an understatement, notwithstanding issues with former CEO Travis Kalanick and the organizational culture he nurtured, described in Chapter 1-21. A competitor to Uber is Lyft, which operates with the same business model.

The taxicab industry was asleep at the wheel. The prices of taxi medallions have crashed, reflecting the huge impact that Uber and Lyft have had on the taxicab industry.

The Lesson Taught by the Failure of Blackberry

From 1999 through 2008, Research in Motion, with its Blackberry smartphone, owned the smartphone market, focused mainly on business users by providing wireless e-mail communication in addition to mobile phone capability. Carrying a Blackberry was somewhat of a status symbol back then. Those who were constantly wedded to their Blackberry were dubbed "Crackberries," including me.

Apple and Google saw an opportunity to develop the consumer market for smartphones. Apple introduced the iPhone in 2007, followed by Google, with its introduction of the Android. Google licensed its Android operating system in 2008 to other smartphone manufacturers such as HTC and Samsung.

Both Apple and Google encouraged independent companies to develop apps that greatly enhanced the user experience, a strategy that Blackberry was late in pursuing, and they never caught up.

Blackberry ignored the competitive challenge of Apple and Android. Did they think that business users would not want to take great photos and then send or text them, or surf the web?

As Apple, Google, and other smartphone manufacturers using the Android operating system captured market share, Blackberry watched in disbelief as they lost their dominant industry position, and now are a nonfactor in the marketplace. I personally switched from a Blackberry to an iPhone in 2011 and never looked back.

With vision and innovation, competitors are developing improved products and services, creatively disrupting manufacturing or application technology, adding new product features, significantly lowering costs, creating new channels of distribution, or changing their industry's business model. They are developing new products or delivering new services that customers don't yet know they need. They are providing a great customer or client experience.

The goal of these companies is to gain a competitive advantage and become the preferred provider of a product or service at your company's expense.

CEOs, learn from Uber, Apple, and Google and anticipate what other innovative companies can do to your industry. Remember, only the paranoid survive. Never rest on your laurels by thinking your company is great. Being paranoid is not only a defensive strategy, but an offensive strategy as well. Be the company that disrupts the market, even if it disrupts your business. Be the company that obsoletes your own products and services. Rather it be you than someone else.

Continuous Improvement Is a Timeless Philosophy

How many of you have experienced initiatives launched by your company's leadership that promised to lead to strong revenue and bottom-line growth, delighted customers, grateful shareholders, and long-term sustainable competitive advantage? How many of these initiatives have delivered the expected results and have been sustainable in the long term?

During my career, management consultants expounded on why their initiative was the "next best thing." These included management by objectives; matrix management; if it's not broke, fix it anyway; total quality management; business process re-engineering; delayering; six sigma; Baldrige Quality Award; Kaizen; and lean manufacturing. Today, you don't hear about many of these initiatives, and depending on your age, have never heard of some of them.

Some of these initiatives lacked substance or never delivered the results intended. Others are bureaucratic and paperwork intensive. When it comes to any form of management initiative, the bottom line is that if your employees don't believe that the benefit is worth the time and effort for the results achieved, it will not be sustainable.

Continuous Improvement

While chief operating officer at PQ Corporation, we found that the one initiative that generated long-term results and was sustainable over time was the philosophy of continuous improvement, or CQI (continuous quality improvement), as we called it within PQ. Why is continuous improvement different than other management initiatives? Instinctively, most employees realize that continuous improvement is needed to grow the company and build a competitive advantage. *To not continually improve means that you fall behind.* No other initiative has this innate imperative.

Even though continuous improvement is led by the CEO and other senior leaders, it is driven by the employees at every level within the company. The senior leadership of the firm is charged with creating an environment where employees develop a sense of ownership in that part of the business in which they work.

This cultural change puts power and responsibility into the hands of employees to initiate improvement projects, without getting upper management's approval. If an improvement idea is beyond their authority level, they are empowered to present the idea to the individual who has the authority to approve it.

Creation of a continuous improvement culture requires training of all managers to be coaches and counselors to their employees, encouraging them to develop and implement their own improvement ideas. Training is also needed to help employees analyze data to determine the root cause of issues, so proper solutions can be identified.

Continuous Improvement Builds Competitive Advantage

By adopting CQI, my company saved millions of dollars from ideas generated and implemented by our employees. Many of these ideas were developed and implemented by the hourly workforce within our plants, using capital funds that they themselves could spend on projects of their choosing. This brought out the creativity in our people, encouraged them to be more proactive, and showed them in a tangible way that they mattered to the success of the company. This helped us be more competitive and provided funds to reinvest in and to grow our business.

So if you are looking for a philosophy to build competitive advantage that is timeless, adopt continuous improvement, led by the CEO but driven by all employees. Companies who do not continually improve will be left behind. Those that do will win the competitive race in the long run.

CHAPTER 2-8

Don't Tell Me
It Can't Be Done!

In the 2001 film *Pearl Harbor*, soon after the United States declares war on Japan following the attack on Pearl Harbor, President Franklin Roosevelt orders the Joint Chiefs of Staff to strike back by bombing Tokyo. These military leaders offer reasons why it can't be done—the U.S. long-range bombers don't have the necessary range from the nearest U.S. base on Midway Island and Russia won't let the United States launch from Russian territory. Roosevelt says to them (YouTube video courtesy of Kreemerz), "*Do not tell me it can't be done.*"[22]

What Roosevelt did was challenge the existing paradigms of his military leaders. He wanted them to be innovative and think out of the box. It took the assistant chief of staff for anti-submarine warfare to do so, an individual you would not necessarily expect to come up with a solution to this challenge. He proposed that B-25 bombers carrying extra fuel be launched off an aircraft carrier that would sail within aircraft striking range of Tokyo. After launch, the carrier would turn back, and after the bombing run, the planes would fly to China and land there.

This bombing mission over Tokyo is enshrined in history as the Doolittle Raid, named for Army Air Corps Lieutenant Colonel James Doolittle, who trained the pilots and led the bombing mission. Even though the mission did little damage to Japan's military capability, it provided a needed boost to American morale, and at the same time showed the Japanese that they were within the reach of American bombers.

When "something can't be done," there is usually a creative path forward that can achieve the result desired, or a similar result that might serve the purpose originally intended.

---

[22] https://youtube.com/watch?v=PFhY6IaUJ40

Your corporate culture must encourage out-of-the-box thinking and risk-taking for this process to take place. Collaboration among people from different operating units, technical disciplines, and business units are sometimes needed to find the path forward, as when the assistant chief of staff for anti-submarine warfare came up with the idea of how to bomb Tokyo.

Rebuilding the Phone System

As manager of operations planning early in my career at PQ Corporation, one of the most impactful lessons I learned was the imperative of breaking paradigms. Paradigms are an established and accepted set of beliefs, and in this context, ways of doing business.

Our CEO, Paul Staley, asked Russell Ackoff, then professor of management at the Wharton School of the University of Pennsylvania, to talk with the senior leadership team at PQ about applying his idealized design approach to our manufacturing technologies to break our paradigms. As a mid-level manager, I was very fortunate to be included in these sessions.

Ackoff described a meeting that he attended in 1951 of engineers and scientists at Bell Labs, a division of the phone company AT&T, in which the facilitator abruptly announced to the meeting participants that the phone system in the United States was just destroyed. How would they not only rebuild the system, but reimagine and improve it? The only criteria that they needed to meet were that the new phone system design had to be technically feasible and operationally viable. The facilitator was asking the meeting participants to break their paradigms and think out of the box.

In the process of establishing the specifications of the new phone system, the participants realized that given the expected growth of phone usage, continued use of the rotary dial phone system in use at the time was not practical. Touch-tone dialing cut 12 seconds off the time it took to dial a phone number and required much less investment than the capital-intensive mechanical rotary dial system currently in place. At that moment in history, the touch-tone dial system became the technology of choice for the future phone system. Little did the participants know the significant impact that a reimagined phone system based on touch-tone dialing would have on our lives in the future.

The Ideal Plant Concept

A number of years later as president of PQ's Industrial Chemicals Group at a meeting with our plant managers, I posed a similar question to the one that was posed by Ackoff at Bell Labs. I told the group that our Augusta, GA, manufacturing plant built many years ago was just destroyed. How would they reimagine, redesign, and build the plant to fulfill the product needs of the plant's customers? The only criteria were that the redesign needed to be technically feasible and operationally viable.

We identified new manufacturing approaches we wanted to include in the new plant design. We subsequently estimated the cost to build and operate the plant and found it would be significantly less using these new technologies.

Our approach to reimagine this plant was called our ideal plant concept, similar to what Ackoff called his idealized design. Whenever capital additions were made to our plants, we considered the risks involved in adopting new technology, and whether we needed to de-risk the decision by applying and testing out the new technology before putting it into commercial practice.

Of course, what is the latest state of the art today will be surpassed by new innovations tomorrow. In addition, this approach fit with our commitment to the continuous improvement of our manufacturing plants, as well as other aspects of our business operations.

Ackoff was considered a pioneer in the field of management science, systems thinking, and operations research. He passed away in 2008. I regret that I did not think to reach out to him in his later years and let him know the significant impact he had on my thinking.

> Leaders, create a culture focused on breaking paradigms. Be familiar with technical advances within your industry so when the opportunity to make process improvements or add manufacturing capacity arises, you know the latest state-of-the-art technology. This is a way to differentiate and create a sustainable advantage over your competitors. And remember, when you hear from employees that something can't be done, respond with "Don't tell me it can't be done. Find a way to do it."

CHAPTER 2-9

Break Paradigms to Build Competitive Advantage

Figure 2-9 Break paradigms through open dialogue, brainstorming and out-of-the-box thinking.

Photo: Sergey Nivens/Getty Images

Breaking paradigms is crucial for achieving breakthrough results. As a business unit general manager, I was taught this lesson by the CEO of our company, Paul Staley, who challenged the design of a new plant my business unit was trying to economically justify. The return on investment was initially below the hurdle rate for this type of project.

Strategically, we wanted to build the plant because it would open a new geography in a growing market for the company and protect that market from the entry of a competitor, but we needed a higher return on investment to get the board's approval. We didn't want to justify the plant just on a strategic basis, but on an economic basis as well.

Think "Out of the Box!"

When I told Staley that the internal rate of return of the project was insufficient to present to the board, he asked that every aspect of the plant design be reviewed with the goal of building the plant at a lower capital cost and running it at a lower operating cost.

This type of plant would normally be staffed by four people on a one-shift operation, led by a plant manager. Staley asked if it would be possible to design a smaller plant to operate with only one person. I said no, that was impossible.

Staley then told me to design the plant with a two-shift self-managed crew without a plant manager—one person on the first shift and one on the second shift, something that had never been done before. My response was, "So, you want a more-efficient plant built at lower capital cost run by fewer people and with no management? These objectives are mutually exclusive!" Staley just smiled and said, "Think out of the box! I know you and your team can do this."

We used the ideal plant model process I described in Chapter 2-7 to reimagine this plant. Working with our engineering and plant operations team, we broke every paradigm we ever had about this type of plant. Through brainstorming, out-of-the-box thinking, and open dialogue, we reoriented equipment and scaled down the capacity of the plant to lower the initial capital investment but left it expandable if and when the demand justified additional capacity. We raised the qualifications of the operators hired to run the plant, ensuring they had the capability to self-manage.

There was much skepticism within the company that the plant could run with a self-managing crew of only two people. For political reasons, I added the cost of a third person to the cash-flow projections. A third person was added a few years later after demand grew, requiring operation on the third shift.

After the plant design was revised and staffing reduced, the return on investment rose significantly, and we received board approval to build the plant. Because of its new design and the way it operated, it was the lowest cost plant of its type in the industry and became our company's model for future plants of this type.

Breaking Paradigms Builds Competitive Advantage

A competitor chose not to enter the geography because of our plant's low-cost operation—they couldn't match its low costs.

A few years later, we built a replica of the plant to serve another geographic market. We operated the plant at even lower cost with one individual on the day shift and a local retiree who filled in when the individual took vacation or a sick day. We fulfilled Paul Staley's original challenge to us: to operate a plant like this with only one person!

How do you create a paradigm-breaking mindset, so it becomes part of the culture of your organization? I believe you need a catalyst and an initiative where existing paradigms can be challenged. You also need an organizational culture where the opinions of all employees on how to achieve breakthrough improvements are valued and where the status quo can be questioned. The organization that accomplishes this will build competitive advantage.

Winning in a Competitive Marketplace

All business leaders face the issue of how to win business in a competitive marketplace. At PQ Corporation, we constantly faced competitive pricing decisions to retain current customers' business as well as win the business of new customers. Price the product or service too low, and you are leaving money on the table. Price it too high, and the customer or client will buy from a competitor.

Many of PQ's customers and the customers of our competitors were supplied under the terms of supply contracts that were one or more years in duration. Before the end of their supply contract, many of these customers would put their business out for bid for the next contract period. In the competitive marketplace, this was an opportunity for us to win a future customer's business currently supplied by a competitor, and an opportunity for a competitor to win the business supplied by our company.

We worked hard to differentiate ourselves on customer and technical service, as did our competition. Price of our commodity products and cost/performance of our specialty and catalyst products played a large factor in whether we won or lost the business.

As a business leader, how do you increase the probability that you will win in the competitive marketplace?

Work To Be the Preferred Provider

At PQ, we were always on the journey to be the preferred provider by providing a great customer experience. We wanted to be the company that every customer would preferentially buy from. Our goal was to help our customers be successful in their businesses by being a great supplier.

Our products always met specifications, our plants were responsive to emergency deliveries, and our sales and customer service people worked to resolve any issues with our account.

At Accounts Served by the Competition, Work to Become a Second Source Provider

When an account's primary provider stubs their toe (and eventually they will—all companies do), as a second source provider, the account is already familiar with your company. Your company could step right in so the account wouldn't suffer an interruption in service. If you provide a great customer/client experience, this will earn you a larger share of the account's business. This is one of the techniques we used at PQ to gain business—become a second source provider and grow share by providing a great customer experience.

Build Strong Customer Relationships

The larger and more strategic the customer, the more we called on them and developed relationships with the leadership hierarchy within the customer's organization.

Our sales representatives "owned" the customer relationship—they were the individuals who kept in frequent touch with their customers to understand trends in their business and any issues they faced with the use of our products. They brought in our knowledgeable technical service people to troubleshoot and resolve issues.

The regional sales manager as well as the national sales manager of our business units would develop relationships up through the customer's organization. When I became the CEO of PQ, I would develop a relationship with my counterpart—the CEO, or if more appropriate, the group president of the business unit purchasing our product.

Get the "Last Phone Call"

If a competitor outbid us, we needed to know about it before the competitor was awarded the business. We wanted the opportunity to convince the customer of the value PQ brought to the supply relationship beyond just the product price, and if necessary, meet the competitive price. That is the value of developing a strong customer relationship—to get the last phone call before the business is awarded.

When I was president of PQ's Canadian subsidiary, we were working on a 10-year contract to supply a pulp and paper mill in Alberta. Our plan was to build a production plant adjacent to the customer to ensure a reliable supply of product.

One afternoon, the business manager responsible for negotiating the supply contract with the customer came into my office in Toronto and told me he just learned that we had competition for the business from a U.S.-based supplier.

This customer was strategic for us. The plant we would build to supply their pulp and paper mill would be strategically placed to supply other pulp mills throughout Alberta. We didn't want this opportunity to go to a competitor. I asked our business manager to make an appointment with the customer's CEO. I wanted to meet with him to close the deal.

We arrived in Alberta the next day and sat across from the CEO and his team. We presented how our company was in the best position to supply not only their product requirements, but also their technical service needs, and how our multiple plants in Canada would be there as backup to provide product to their plant.

We didn't need to cut the price we originally offered. All we needed to do was freeze the price for three years, something the U.S. competitor wouldn't do. At the end of the meeting, the CEO and I looked each other in the eye, stood up, and shook hands across the table. I knew we had a deal.

Without the relationship previously established by our business manager and the nonmonetary value we could deliver to the customer, in addition to being able to freeze the price for three years, I am not sure we would have prevailed in winning the business.

Be Dedicated to Continuous Improvement

In PQ's commodity chemical business, where our products and those of our competitors are the same chemically, price was an important competitive differentiator. A strong commitment to continuous improvement to drive costs down was critical to the ability to compete.

In our specialty chemicals and catalyst businesses, where our products and those of the competition are differentiated based on product cost/performance, this metric must continually improve at a pace greater than that of competition.

Continuous improvement can be incremental or stepwise, with large improvements based on innovation and a change in paradigms. This permits greater pricing flexibility than a competitor, whose improvements may lag, and is key to long-term competitive success.

When going up against a competitor, you want them to think, "Oh no. Not those guys." That's how good you want to be. That's how you win business in a competitive marketplace.

CHAPTER 2-11

When Making Decisions, "Avoid Going to Abilene"

How often have you faced a situation within your organization where the decision-making process was not effective in determining the best course of action? When the results are less than what is desired, everyone wonders, "Why did we proceed down this path? Why weren't alternatives fully considered?"

In his 1974 book, *The Abilene Paradox: The Management of Agreement*, Jerry B. Harvey, professor emeritus of management at George Washington University, describes a situation where a father-in-law suggests to his family that they all drive to Abilene for dinner, and everyone agrees.

No one shared their reservations about going to Abilene, so off they went. After having a terrible meal, each family member reveals that they personally thought that the other members of the family wanted to go, and therefore did not express opposition to the suggestion.

Constructive Conflict Is Important in All Organizations

Harvey writes,[23] "The inability to manage agreement, not the inability to manage conflict, is the essential symptom that defines organizations caught in the web of the Abilene Paradox."

Many companies face decisions that are more complex than the example described above, with ramifications significantly more impactful than a bad meal. How do you cultivate a culture within your organization to avoid the Abilene paradox and other more serious flaws in the decision-making process?

---

[23] https://assets.aspeninstitute.org/content/uploads/files/content/upload/16-Harvey-Abilene-Paradox-redacted.pdf

Whether the leader is the CEO of a large organization or a subunit of that organization, the quality of the decision-making process will depend on the organizational culture established by the leader. Direct reports quickly pick up on that culture and how the leader responds to contrary points of view.

It Is Critical for a Leader to Welcome Open Discussion and Ask for Opinions

When the leader welcomes opinions, better ideas often emerge—different than those originally considered—allowing for a superior decision to be made.

When a leader expresses an opinion on a course of action early in a discussion, it is more difficult for alternatives suggested by their team to be seriously considered. This is especially the case when the leader has a reputation for being opinionated and doesn't listen to other points of view. Consequently, meaningful discussion does not occur, and the best strategy may not be pursued.

A leader should hold back their personal opinion until the team members have presented their ideas. This should also be a time for leaders to listen to their direct reports and see how they approach the situation.

After discussing an important decision, come back to it in a few days to allow team members to reflect on their individual positions on the subject. During this period, team members may alter their position on an issue. Never criticize anyone for changing their mind.

Beware of the comment, "We need to move fast on this." It should send up red flags and should not force a decision before the ramifications are carefully considered.

The worst thing for any organization is to have it populated by "yes-people," or those who are reluctant to express their views, especially if they are contrary to the thinking of the leader, or of the group.

The Importance of Lone Wolfs

Having a contrary view when everyone else is leaning in one direction on an issue is difficult, but necessary to arrive at the best decision. These individuals may be labeled as not being team players, so it takes courage to be the lone wolf.

The view of the contrarian may not be adopted, but that view provides an alternative to which the popular view can be tested and confirmed as the best course of action.

How lone wolves express their contrary views is important to whether or not they are considered, as well as to their credibility within the team.

Value the lone wolf. Consider what they have to say. You will increase the probability of making the right decisions for your business.

CHAPTER 2-12

To Improve Results, Benchmark Sister Operations

Figure 2-12 Encourage internal benchmarking to improve business results.

Photo: People Images Collection/ Getty Images

I recently attended a conference at which the general manager of a business unit within a large company described how he was able to achieve a significant turnaround in the operating results of his organization. He broke all accepted paradigms about what was possible.

After his presentation, I asked how other general managers within his company were at applying his approach to improve the results of their business units. He responded that although he was willing to share his approach, no other general manager bothered to benchmark what he did to achieve the turnaround. He said there wasn't a culture within the company to benchmark other operating units.

Benchmarking competitors is important to determine a company's competitiveness in the marketplace and learn about best practices within the industry. However, it can be a difficult process to benchmark competitors due to the frequent inability to get the data that is needed. Internally benchmarking sister operations that are achieving great results within the company is much easier. The data is available. So why isn't it done as a matter of course?

Internal Benchmarking Is Not Part of the Corporate Culture

As with many other techniques to improve operating performance, such as the process of continuous improvement, delivering a great customer experience, or empowering employees to make decisions, internal benchmarking is not part of the leadership mindset in some organizations. The CEO needs to be held accountable by the board to bring this mindset to the company and make it part of its culture.

Bonuses Are Based on Business Unit Results Only

If there is no incentive to share what works across all business units, a huge opportunity is wasted. Occasionally, business units view themselves to be in competition with each other. *The shareholders don't care about the results of individual operating units. They care about the results of the entire company.*

Bonuses should be based on both individual operating unit results and corporate results, so there is an incentive for sharing what works within other operating units. When benchmarking improves the results of a business, it needs to be celebrated throughout the company to encourage more internal benchmarking.

"By Helping You, I Diminish My Own Chance for Career Advancement"

Unfortunately, some business unit leaders feel that they are playing a zero-sum game: "If I help to make you look good, I will not look as good." It needs to be made clear that in fact this attitude diminishes one's chances of career advancement and will have a negative impact on the individual's performance review. The desire to help others within the company should have a positive impact on one's chances for advancement.

"It Is a Weakness to Apply Successful Techniques Developed by Others"

Business unit leaders who feel that benchmarking others diminishes their own stature lose out on opportunities to improve their operating unit's results and limit their chances to advance.

Using the ideas and applying the techniques of others shows you are open-minded and are not limited by the "not invented here syndrome," which is universally frowned upon by all effective leaders.

Some Business Unit Leaders Are Not Comfortable with Change

There is a universal expectation that all leaders will move their areas of responsibility forward and not be wedded to the status quo. Leaders who resist change shouldn't be in their jobs and need to be replaced.

Internal benchmarking and operational improvement need to be key components of any organization's culture. It builds competitive advantage.

PART 3

Advancing Your Career: Get Out of Your Comfort Zone. You Never Know Where the Future Will Take You

Be Different Than Your Peers

Figure 3-1 *Prospective employers will want to know if you are a good fit. Conversely, you should determine if the culture of a prospective employer is a good fit for you.*

Photo: Portis Head1 Collection/Getty Images

People advance in their careers by differentiating themselves from their peers, just as businesses differentiate themselves from their competitors. An individual's track record of accomplishments, skills, and experience gained in previous jobs can be used to achieve that peer differentiation.

Recently, I had lunch with a college sophomore at Drexel University who was just finishing up her first of three full time six-month co-op assignments at a company before returning to campus for classes. This is an opportunity for students to gain valuable hands-on experience at as many as three companies in different fields. I asked her what she had learned during her co-op job and what she contributed to the organization.

She responded with the many ideas she offered to improve the organization's business processes. Because her suggestions fell on deaf ears, she thought her experiences at this company would not help build her resume, which is one of the most important things anyone can do regardless of where one is in their career.

I told her to the contrary, her focus on continuous improvement is exactly what might make her resume stand out from the dozens submitted for a job opening and get her an interview. A commitment to continuous improvement, among other factors, is a differentiator for any job candidate.

Are You Results Oriented?

In a job interview, you will be asked about the results that you achieved in your previous positions. How did those results support the goals of your organization, or those of a customer or client? Show how you have been innovative and have exercised initiative. A potential employer will assess what you can do for their company, based on what you accomplished at your previous employer.

Are You Customer/Client Focused?

All employees have internal and/or external customers/clients. If you are in a staff position, your job is to help other staff and line units within your company be successful in achieving their goals. If you are in a line position, your job is to help your company's clients or customers be successful in their businesses. How have you done so?

The Holy Grail of any business is to be the preferred provider to its market and the company that customers/clients will first choose to purchase products or services from. How have you helped your previous employer travel the journey to be the preferred provider to its market?

Do You Embrace Continuous Improvement?

In your previous jobs, if you felt there was a more effective approach to accomplishing your organization's goals, did you challenge paradigms and the accepted ways of doing things within your area of responsibility? Challenging the status quo shows initiative and your desire to improve the company's operation.

What Is Your Leadership Style?

You should share your expectations and jointly develop goals with your direct reports without micromanaging how those goals are achieved. You should help create a sense of ownership in your employees for what they do and hold them accountable for results.

Are You Effective at Selling Your Ideas?

People who are in sales aren't the only ones who sell. Everyone is selling their ideas to their boss, their peers, the teams they serve on, and their direct reports. This requires good presentation skills. It also requires good listening skills, not only to address objections, but to be open to other ideas. Discuss how you have sold your ideas to your organization and demonstrate that you listen and value the opinions of others.

Do You Fit the Culture?

Prospective employers will want to know if you are a good fit. Conversely, you will want to determine if the culture of a prospective employer is a good fit for you. Stay away from a company that has a reputation for unethical dealings with employees or with customers, or has a toxic culture.

The key to landing your next job is differentiating yourself, demonstrating that you are an effective leader, and developing a reputation of achieving results within your field. Do this well, and employers will seek you out.

CHAPTER 3-2

How to Build Your Personal Brand

All of us are familiar with a business brand. It's the marketplace recognition of the promise of a company or professional services firm to meet or exceed the high expectations of its customers or clients in the delivery of products or services. Less familiar is a personal brand, which is the recognized promise of an individual with talent, expertise and experience to help a client or employer to be successful in their business.

Customers and clients buy from companies with strong brands, such as Nike, Mercedes-Benz, Apple, Google, and Starbucks, to name a few. These companies have a reputation for consistently offering high-quality products or services and delivering a great customer experience.

Companies with a great brand reputation are often not the lowest price offering in the marketplace, but offer perceived value for the price charged. The strength of their brand gives these companies a competitive advantage. They become the preferred provider in their marketplace. They are the companies that customers and clients want to do business with, and they hold a significant market share.

The same holds true for personal brands. Individuals develop a reputation such that clients want to do business with them. Employers want to promote them to their next job within the company or hire them as new employees. They differentiate themselves and develop a competitive advantage over their peers.

Ram V. Iyer of The Business Institute writes, [23]

Personal branding is the intentional identification, packaging and marketing of a person's mission, strengths, capabilities, talents, background, appearance, and so on, as a brand. A big objective of personal branding is to establish a specific image or impression of the person in the mind of others that evokes positive emotions.

Iyer continues,

If you build a strong personal brand, the benefits could increase your popularity, credibility, prestige, customer loyalty and market differentiation; it could attract new (and the right) clients, partners, employees and build bigger networks; and it could increase your perceived value (ability to charge higher prices) in the marketplace.

So, as an individual, how do you build your personal brand?

Do Your Job and Do It Well!

Develop a reputation within your company, client base and industry, as someone who achieves results, is a problem solver and facilitator with high emotional intelligence, is an individual who improves business processes, and is someone who brings people together to find common ground.

Develop Your Reputation as a Thought Leader, a Recognized Authority in Your Field of Expertise

Get what you have accomplished and are accomplishing out in front of an audience. Volunteer to speak in front of groups. Help others be successful.

Write articles or blogs on LinkedIn. Develop a website that can feature your articles and share your views. Exercise caution not to criticize the company at which you work or its leaders, and never reveal confidential

---

[23] https://businessthinking.com/blog/personal-branding

information. Build an e-mail list of individuals who would be interested in what you convey and send them what you write.

Develop a Reputation for Honesty and Integrity

Reputation is defined by Merriam-Webster as "overall quality or character as seen or judged by people in general." Reputation is within the top 30 percent of words searched on the Merriam-Webster website.

Ethics, meanwhile, is in the top 1 percent of words searched, indicating its importance within our society. People do not want to work for or deal with leaders or companies whose reputations are tarnished or who are not ethical.

Reputation and ethics are among key determinants of how successful you will be. People will not want to do business with those they don't trust.

Hone Your Leadership Skills

Become known as an individual who creates a culture in which employees are empowered and encouraged to develop a sense of ownership in what they do. Develop a reputation for holding people accountable for results, as well as a leader people want to work for. Become known as someone who develops future leaders.

Always Have and Project the Right Attitude

Attitude is a significant determinant of your success. *Develop a reputation for seeing a world of possibilities and abundance, versus seeing limitations and scarcity. Individuals with positive attitudes move forward in their career. Those with a negative attitude do not.*

Be on a journey to be the best in the world at what you do. Follow the above advice to build your personal brand. It will help you advance your career, especially when in transition to your next job. When employers vet potential new employees, they look for the traits identified above.

Selling Your Ideas Is the Key to Professional Advancement

Have you ever given any thought to how to sell your ideas to others, and the most effective way to do so? The "art of selling" is usually associated with the selling of a product or service. This view is much too narrow, as we are also selling our ideas to others. Our ability to get others to buy into our ideas and initiatives and rally them to our cause is a prime determinant for a successful career. No matter what your profession, no matter your level within your organization, you are always selling your ideas.

The late Lee Iacocca, the former chairman of the board of Chrysler Corporation, said, "You can have brilliant ideas, but if you can't get them across, your ideas won't get you anywhere."[24] How true.

Leaders cannot just announce a new initiative and expect it to be adopted without convincing those within their organization that there is merit to their idea. Depending on the initiative, they may need the support of their boss, peers, and direct reports. Leaders need to help create a sense of need and a feeling of ownership in employees for the initiative, so they are committed to its success. So, how do you sell your ideas? How do you influence others to pursue your initiatives?

Be Effective in Presenting Your Ideas

When making a PowerPoint presentation, ensure that the audience can read your slides. I have attended many conferences at which experts in their fields made presentations where the fonts on their slides were too small to be read, or so much information was packed on each slide to render it undecipherable. This hurt the credibility of the presenter.

---

[24] https://quotes.net/quote/7

Always place yourself in the position of the audience of what you are presenting, either via PowerPoint of verbally, and ask yourself, is this an effective presentation?

Your Idea Should Focus on the Needs of Your Customer or Client

Your idea is more likely to have better reception if you focus how it benefits customers or clients, improves a business process, fulfills a need, or solves a problem of the individual to whom you are selling the idea.

What is in it for them: financial gain, societal benefit, or fulfilling their desire to leave a legacy to future generations? Find out and position your idea to garner interest and commitment.

Have you fully evaluated the idea you are selling, and can you articulate responses to probing questions? Some questions one should consider are:

- What are the benefits of the idea and its return on investment?
- What are the risks, and are they acceptable?
- Do the benefits outweigh the risks?
- What is the cost to implement the idea, and is the cost within the ability of the organization to absorb?
- What are the alternatives, including the alternative of doing nothing?
- What are the risks of doing nothing, and are those costs too high to bear?
- What happens if the idea fails?

Are You Fully Convinced of the Merits of Your Idea?

If you are not convinced of the idea's merits, you will never have sufficient conviction to convince others. If the idea fails, you will be held accountable because your name is on it. Therefore, you need to be convinced that the idea will work. If the idea is a good one but there are some issues, talk through the issues to minimize risk.

Approach the Individual to Whom You Want to Sell an Idea When They Are Not Distracted

Don't raise the subject unless you feel that you can have their full attention. Watch for eye contact. Not maintaining eye contact is an indication they are not interested and not absorbing what you are saying. If you sense that the message is not impactful to the individual you are speaking with, change the messaging. Be aware of how you and your idea are being received.

If You Need to Sell an Initiative, First Speak to Group Members Individually

By explaining the initiative in one-on-one conversations, you have a chance to gauge reactions and address any concerns. You might also get good advice on modifying the initiative to increase its attractiveness or probability of success. If you first introduce the initiative to the group without laying any groundwork with the group's members, the group may respond with a negative reaction without thoughtful consideration.

Do You Have Credibility?

When you are selling ideas, you are selling yourself. Within any organization, those with the highest credibility and trust will have an easier time having their ideas considered and accepted.

- Do people have confidence in you?
- Does the team trust you?
- How do you earn trust? Be transparent, admit failures, don't blame others for your mistakes, and always meet your commitments to others.
- How do you build credibility? Develop a reputation and a track record of success with previous initiatives.

There are people who don't want to engage in the process of selling ideas, or don't have ideas to sell. Some people simply don't like change, and don't realize that change is a constant in life. This is unfortunate. These individuals are missing out on an opportunity to influence their organization. When they are searching for their next job, they will not have in their background what is most valued by a new employer. They will have no track record of contributions that drove their former organization forward.

CHAPTER 3-4

Successfully Navigate Office Politics

Throughout my career, I have watched the game of office politics play out in many organizations, including my own. Office politics can have negative implications for the people playing the game, their co-workers, and the organization itself.

Traits of Those Who Play Office Politics

Some people feel that the only way they can advance within an organization is at the expense of others to make themselves look good, while making others look bad. They deflect responsibility and often blame others—both peers and subordinates—for their own failures.

They take undo credit for the success of initiatives beyond their contributions and misrepresent the facts to cast themselves in a favorable light. They are good at "managing up." To the senior leadership of the organization, they heap criticism on their peers. They destroy trust, and when trust is destroyed, the organization becomes toxic and dysfunctional.

I have often wondered why any boss puts up with the actions of employees who play office politics. Either they are blind to it or think that they will achieve better results as is, rather than if the organization performed as a high-performance team in which employees trusted each other. They are wrong.

Bosses might counsel employees who play office politics to get them to change, with mixed results. The employee will often deny their destructive behavior. Many times, their behavior is due to their personality. They won't change. That's who they are.

The Importance of Tone and Culture

Those managers who undercut their peers and play political games are setting the wrong tone and nurturing the wrong culture, which will be emulated by those within their group, undermining trust with employees in other groups. Silos are created and information is not shared, to the detriment of the entire organization.

As part of every manager's performance review, their tone and culture need to be assessed, including that of the CEO. If the tone and culture are wrong, regardless of whether the manager is currently achieving results, those results will not be sustainable long term.

Eventually, employees who play office politics are recognized for who they are and the damage they cause. They are either terminated or depart on their own when their political gamesmanship has been uncovered and is no longer useful to them at their current company.

So, as an employee within an organization, how should you defend against those who are playing political games to undermine you?

Keep Your Adversaries Close

There is an old saying, "Keep your friends close, and your enemies closer,"[25] ascribed by some to Chinese general and military strategist Sun Tzu in his book *The Art of War* (circa 400 BC), and by others to the 16th-century political philosopher Niccolo Machiavelli in his book *The Prince* (circa 1513). This saying can also be applied to office politics.

By keeping your adversaries close, you can get insight into what they are doing and thinking. You also have the opportunity to sway their thinking and show them that undermining you is not a productive use of their time. You may be able to co-op them and get them to be one of your supporters rather than a detractor. However, once they violate your trust, you may never fully trust them again. Once lost, trust is very difficult to regain.

---

[25] http://quotationspage.com/quote/36994.html

How To Be Successful in a Political Environment

On various occasions during my career, I have been the subject of political attacks by others. Did I ever confront the individual? No. I felt that would be counterproductive. Whether or not to confront someone is a personal decision and depends on each individual situation.

How did I successfully cope with these attacks? I built a strong informal organization through which I got things accomplished. I built alliances with others by helping them accomplish their objectives. Through these alliances, I was made aware of political attacks that were not visible to me. I did the same for those with whom I had developed alliances. Did this strategy work? Ultimately, I was the one who rose up through the organization, not them.

So, how can you rise above office politics? Meet your commitments to others. Build trust with your peers. Develop alliances. Keep your adversaries close. Build political capital. Most importantly, do your job and achieve results, and let those results speak for themselves.

Never Violate the Trust That Others Have in You

All relationships revolve around trust. As you are promoted, you are given increased responsibility and are trusted to act in a responsible manner. Not only are you trusted by the senior leadership of the company and your customers or clients, but also indirectly by the company's stockholders to act with integrity and in an ethical manner. Never violate that trust.

I am familiar with a situation in which an individual was promoted up through the organization to the level of general manager of a division selling services which were priced-out by job. The company discovered that he was overcharging customers for the work performed in order to artificially pump up the revenues and bottom-line results of his division, which increased his bonus opportunity.

When the customers discovered they were being overcharged, they stopped buying from that division. Word spread throughout the industry, adversely impacting business with other customers. As orders dwindled, employees started to leave the company to take jobs elsewhere. The division eventually closed, harming the company and its investors.

The general manager tainted his reputation, which will impact his future employment prospects. Did he think he would never get caught?

Everyone is familiar with the saying, "trust but verify." Regardless of the controls in place and the efforts of internal auditors, not all unethical acts will be discovered before the damage is done. When you are hired, the company assumes that you are trustworthy. Never violate that trust. Always act with integrity and in an ethical manner. Your good name is priceless. Always protect it.

Dealing with Toxic People in the Workplace

At some point in our careers, many of us will find ourselves working with bosses, direct reports, or peers who lack ethics and integrity. These people are toxic and hinder the organization's ability to achieve its objectives.

Toxic people will throw others who stand in their way under the proverbial bus for their own purpose of advancing through the organization at the expense of others. They will criticize colleagues behind their backs to undermine them.

Those who are toxic are not trusted by their peers or direct reports. The actions of everyone they work with have a defensive component, which hinders any group from becoming a high-performance team. Toxic people within the organization don't realize that their personal integrity, reputation, and character is a valuable asset. It determines if people want to deal with them.

Toxic people are good at managing up, so their behavior may not be transparent to their boss. Everyone hopes that sooner or later they will be terminated.

So, what do you do if:

You Work for a Toxic Boss

Do your job and do it well. You may not be permitted to make many decisions without the boss's approval, so overcommunicate to make sure you are both on the same page.

Ensure you are part of an informal network within your organization. It's a source of mutual support on developing strategies to deal with toxic individuals.

You may decide to transfer to another position within the organization or leave the company. Or, you may decide to wait until your toxic boss leaves the company or is fired. You need to weigh your alternatives and decide on your personal course of action.

I once worked for this type of boss and learned how to deal with him. One day, he was ranting about an issue, and I politely told him that I was going to leave his office. I said that when he calmed down and could discuss the issue in a rational way, we would talk again. I told him he could come to my office or call me back to his office to discuss the issue.

I don't think anyone had ever said anything like that to him before. And yes, I was concerned about being fired for insubordination, but it was one of those moments when I had to change the dynamic between us. Twenty minutes later, he came to my office and in a calm and business-like manner, we discussed and decided on a strategy to resolve the issue at hand. He never treated me poorly again.

I was eventually promoted out of that manager's organization, and then promoted again and became his boss. He continued to treat the people in his organization poorly, so I fired him. The employees within that organization celebrated for days.

You Work with a Toxic Peer

As in the case of working for a toxic boss, do your job and do it well, and develop informal alliances with others. They are a great source of information as to what your toxic peer is saying about you. Be on guard for criticism of your work behind your back. Don't play the same game as your toxic peer. Let your results speak to the quality of your work.

You Have a Toxic Direct Report

I discuss this situation in Chapter 1-15 titled "Do You Have a Tyrant Reporting to You?" *What should you do if a tyrant is one of your direct reports? Don't tolerate it. If the individual doesn't rapidly change, you need to part company with them for the betterment of your team and organization.*

If you are a toxic individual, you need to realize that your behavior will not lead to sustainable success. Eventually you will be terminated, and your reputation ruined. No one will trust you nor want to work with you. There is a valuable adage, "Never burn your bridges." So true.

Want to Learn CEO Skills? Become an Entrepreneur

Visit a college entrepreneurship fair and you will interact with students developing the skills of a CEO. This was my recent experience attending the two-day Startup Fest of the Charles D. Close School of Entrepreneurship at Drexel University, the first free-standing, degree-granting school of entrepreneurship in the United States.

Since the Close School of Entrepreneurship was founded in 2014, its faculty has taught over 4,000 students majoring in nearly every course of study across the university.

At Startup Fest, students throughout Drexel showcased the businesses they are building. These students are not only learning entrepreneurship skills, but also important skills as the leaders of their fledgling businesses.

Entrepreneurship Students Learn the Skills of CEOs in Real Time

These entrepreneurs are honing their elevator pitches, developing business strategies, choosing partners, hiring their first employees, building their teams, raising funds from investors, protecting their intellectual property, choosing channels of distribution, and dealing with customers.

They are also learning how to de-risk their decisions and manage a P&L statement. They are learning these skills in real time and risking their own or their investor's funds. These are the skills and responsibilities of all CEOs.

I asked these entrepreneurs to describe the market they were aiming to penetrate, how they would compete with other companies currently in the market, and how they would differentiate their product or service so their business would attract customers. I asked them, "Why will people want to buy from you?" This focuses entrepreneurs on the most import-ant question that will determine the success or failure of their business.

Students starting businesses are learning to be leaders in an environ-ment where their decisions have real monetary consequences—much dif-ferent than learning from case studies while sitting in a classroom. Many graduates don't get the opportunity to lead people or experience these wide range of responsibilities until well into their careers.

Entrepreneurship training teaches you the importance of focus, per-severance, and tenacity in pursuing a goal, getting out of your comfort zone, and how to pivot to another course of action when it appears you are proceeding down a dead end. It also teaches how to overcome or go around obstacles.

Future bosses may say, "Don't tell me it can't be done. Find a way to do it." You learn to exhaust all possibilities as an entrepreneur before deciding to pivot. One learns how to handle inevitable failure, and how to recover and try again. The adage, "Anyone who has never made a mistake has never tried anything new" is true. Mistakes are inevitable. What is important is what you have learned from them.

These students also gain a certain mindset and develop skills that are use-ful whether they start a business or work for a start-up or an established com-pany. This mindset and these skills will help differentiate them from their peers within their current company when going for a promotion or when applying for their next job at a different company.

Entrepreneurship Students Learn Selling and Networking Skills

Starting a business teaches students how to sell their ideas to others, both verbally and through graphical presentations, something all of us will be doing our entire careers regardless of our position within an organization. Entrepreneurship students get real-life feedback on whether their selling skills are effective and can adjust them based on that feedback.

Entrepreneurs learn networking skills due to the numerous interac-tions they have with a variety of people. These skills are critical to career success. Future jobs are most likely to come from one's network, and the ability to effectively expand that network will help one land that next job. More on networking in Chapter 3-10.

My advice to all college students: If you can obtain entrepreneurship train-ing, do so. It will differentiate you among your peers, which will make you more attractive to future employers.

Even if one eventually works for an established company, the mindset and skills learned as an entrepreneur are invaluable to an individual's success. It sets them apart from others and is a sig-nificant differentiator that will help that individual compete for a promotion or their next job.

Be Aware of the Unintended Consequences of Your Decisions

Nearly all of us have heard the term "unintended consequences," but we may not be aware of how to avoid them. In February 2018, in the publication *The Library of Economics and Liberty*, Robert Norton wrote,[26] "The law of unintended consequences, often cited but rarely defined, is that actions of people—and especially of government—always have effects that are unanticipated or unintended."

When the unintended consequence of a decision is favorable, there is never an issue. When the unintended consequence is adverse, depending on its impact, the decision-making process is questioned, as is the leader who made the decision.

In his article, Norton wrote about sociologist Robert Merton, who in 1935 identified the causes of unintended consequences, three of which are in the control of the decision maker. I would like to focus on these three causes: ignorance, error, and immediacy of interest.

Ignorance and Error

In both of these cases, leaders make decisions on issues without considering the unintended consequences or before needed information is obtained. These are decisions that are not well thought out nor operationalized.

During my tenure as the CEO of PQ Corporation, I sat through meetings at which the management of a business unit presented their

---

[26] https://econlib.org/library/Enc/UnintendedConsequences.html

plan to enter a new market, with no consideration of the unintended consequence of a competitive response and how it would impact our company's market entry. I would ask:

- Is the market growing at a sufficient rate to absorb a new supplier without a competitive response?
- Will competitors respond by price cutting, or in a different way?
- What differentiates our product in the marketplace to limit a competitive response? Why would customers stop buying from their incumbent supplier and decide to buy from our company?

A leader will often need to make a decision, but the information desired to make a fully informed decision is not available. Before making that decision, effective leaders listen to the opinions of their experts and they fall back on their own experience, common sense, and good critical judgment. This is how they de-risk a decision and minimize the chance of unintended consequences.

Immediacy of Interest

Merton describes this third type of decision as when "someone wants the intended consequence of an action so much that he purposefully chooses to ignore any unintended effects," to the peril of the decision maker and the organization.

In Chapter 1-5, I describe NASA's decision to launch the space shuttle *Challenger* on January 28, 1986 in cold weather, against the advice of the Thiokol engineers, who were concerned about the brittleness of the solid rocket booster O-rings. This is an example of a decision driven by immediacy of interest. NASA had promised Congress an aggressive and unrealistic launch frequency. The pressure to meet this schedule resulted in a catastrophic decision to launch the *Challenger* in cold temperature conditions, well below the ambient temperature for which the solid rocket booster O-rings were designed.

What is the cause of immediacy of interest type decisions? Certainly, hubris is one. Dictionary.com defines hubris as "excessive pride or self-confidence, arrogance." Arrogant leaders are rarely successful over the long term.

Another cause of immediacy of interest decisions is the pressure to act, which in and of itself is a way of achieving results. However, at what risk and at what cost? How many times do we read in the press about unethical or illegal acts that were committed due to the pressure to get something done? These situations eventually almost always become public, adversely impacting the reputations of the individuals and the organizations involved. The reputations of organizations recover over time. Those of the individuals rarely do.

How do you avoid immediacy of interest decisions? If you are the boss, set high expectations for achieving great results, but make it clear to the organization that it must be done in an honest and ethical manner, and unintended consequences must be considered. No other way is acceptable.

Surround yourself with people who will tell you what they think, not what you want to hear. Listen to your experts. They know more about the unintended consequences than you do. And remember, what you do reflects not only on you, but on your organization and your colleagues as well. Don't let them down.

CHAPTER 3-9

Push Through Your Self-Perceived Limitations

Figure 3-9 Get out of your comfort zone. Those who have never failed have never tried anything new.

Photo: Coompia77 Collection/Getty Images

Why do some people experience various degrees of success over the course of their careers while others experience less success? During my career, I have observed many successful people and those wanting to achieve success. There are those who succumb to their self-perceived limitations and those who find a way to push through them.

The statement "Whether you think you can or can't, you're right"[27] is ascribed to Henry Ford. Your attitude and your ability to push through self-perceived limitations play key roles in how successful you will be.

My Personal Experience Pushing Through Self-Perceived Limitations

A friend at my gym, Patti Morris, drove this home for me. I had been doing assisted pull-ups on an exercise machine that uses counterweights because I believed I did not have sufficient upper-body strength to do pull-ups without them. She came up to me and said, "I know you can do pull-ups unassisted."

I told her that I hadn't done unassisted pull-ups since high school and I couldn't do them now. She egged me on, challenging me to do just one. By now, a crowd was gathering, and I felt huge peer pressure to try to do one pull-up. I walked over to the machine without counterweights and, with my friends watching, nervously jumped up six inches and grabbed the pull-up bar. To my surprise, I was able to do two!

I never used the counterweight machine again. Over subsequent months, I pushed hard and worked my way up to three sets of 10 unassisted pull-ups. I learned a valuable lesson from my friend: You are only limited by your own self-perceived limitations. Thank you, Patti Morris!

Sometimes it takes a friend, colleague, coach, or mentor to inspire you to the next level. When you move to that next level, you never look back, you only look forward. As leaders, our job is to inspire others around us—to help them move to that next level.

Take on New Challenges

You differentiate yourself among your peers by trying new things, sometimes failing, but moving on and continuing to try something new. This

---

[27] https://allbusiness.com/whether-you-think-you-can-or-cant-youre-right-henry-ford-3874550-1.html

trait will help you land your next job. Employers hire those who embrace change, rather than those who don't.

The type of company at which you want to work values employees who are not afraid to innovate, embrace change, and, yes, occasionally make mistakes and learn from them.

Your attitude, which is apparent to everyone you interface with, plays a significant role in your success. Be a person who sees a world of abundance and possibilities, not one who sees a world of limitations and scarcity. Push through self-perceived limitations. You never know what the future holds or where it will take you.

A Lesson in the Power of Networking

The power of networking came into sharp focus for me when I was able to introduce a student of the Pennoni Honors College of Drexel University to a C-suite executive at eBay.

After speaking with a group of students at a lunch and learn event on how to develop into effective leaders as their careers progress, one of the students introduced herself and shared her goal to work in Silicon Valley in the area of communications and marketing after graduation. She asked me if I knew anyone she could network with in that field in Silicon Valley.

I immediately thought of Richelle Parham, chief marketing officer of eBay at the time (and a Drexel alum). Within hours, I connected the student to Parham.

All students should be taught the power of networking, so they are comfortable introducing themselves to individuals that might be helpful in developing their careers. This student had the initiative to introduce herself to me and ask if I could help her make a Silicon Valley connection. Had the student not had that initiative, the introduction would not have occurred.

Networking can take you in unexpected directions. It can change your life, and perhaps enable you to help change the lives of others.

Networking enables us to meet new people, introduces us to new ideas and perspectives, and helps us consider new approaches to problems. It provides a way to benchmark others and discuss best practices within your industry. Networking builds communities of individuals who have similar or related interests. Members of networks provide assistance to each other, and eventually trust develops within the community. You are more apt to do business with a member of your network because they will strive to meet your expectations so you will recommend them to others, both within and outside of your community.

As a leader, networking should be a consistent practice because you never know when you might need a resource to help you or your team. Many jobs are filled through referrals. Everyone should develop networking skills because you never know when you will need to go to your network to find your next job.

How Can You Effectively Network and Develop Networking Skills?

- Always be out and about meeting new people.
- At an event, learn how to join a group conversation and how to graciously depart the group to meet other people at the event.
- Recognize people in serious conversation and know when not to interrupt them.
- Learn how to start conversations with those you have not previously met.
- Practice sharing what you do in a few sentences (the proverbial elevator speech).
- Don't dominate conversations. Make good eye contact, be a good listener, and show interest by asking relevant questions.
- Look for common areas and subjects that can form the basis of a future conversation and relationship.

Obtain an e-mail address to thank the individual you are networking with and include something that you both spoke about so you are memorable and can differentiate yourself among others that the individual met that day.

Networking is one of the most powerful tools you can use to further develop your career and grow your business, regardless of whether you are a college student, business owner, or CEO of a company. It will also help you develop your interpersonal skills. Networking is a skill that should be taught to all students, regardless of area of study.

Learn How to Mitigate Risks and Deal with Failure

For those of us who have a lifetime of business and leadership experiences, it is an honor to be invited to share those experiences with the future generation of leaders. At the invitation of Dr. Barrie Litzky, associate professor at the Charles D. Close School of Entrepreneurship of Drexel University, I spoke to two of her undergraduate entrepreneurship classes, titled Ready, Set, Fail.

Quoting from the Close School course catalogue description: "There are many students who say they want to be an entrepreneur, but they are often not ready for the risk that comes with starting and growing a business. Taking risks requires a deep appreciation of failure."

This course is about how to deal with and recover from failure—something we all need to learn. Taking risks with occasional failure is a natural part of life. If student entrepreneurs are taught how to de-risk their decisions, they will have a higher propensity for taking risks.

When pursuing a new initiative, you should commit resources in a planned, stepwise fashion at a pace commensurate with the pace of success of the initiative. This de-risks your project and conserves resources in the event the path to success requires you to pivot to another approach.

Two key things to remember: Never make the same mistake twice, and never make a mistake that can sink your company.

How Well Do You Know the Market?

Whether one is an entrepreneur, works for a start-up or for an established company, consider the following questions as you plan your new initiative:

- Does the market need the product or service you're developing?

- If the product or service already exists in the marketplace, does the differentiation between what you are developing and what currently exists in the market provide sufficient incentive to get customers to evaluate what you have developed and get them to switch?
- If the product or service is new and future customers or clients don't yet know they need what you are developing, how will you convince them that they need it?
- Have you performed market research on your new product? Conducted customer focus groups? Sold prototypes and gauged customer acceptance?

You should always be asking: "Why will customers or clients buy my product or service?"

Imagine What Could Go Wrong, and How You Would Mitigate It

Andy Grove, the former chairman and CEO of chip maker Intel, once said, "Only the paranoid survive." Every business leader thinks about what could go wrong and what the proper reaction might be. In the case of entrepreneurs, they may need to pivot quickly and take a different approach if they hit an impediment.

Can the introduction of a new product to the marketplace be phased in, so the capital and resources required are not invested all at once but over time, allowing for adjustments in strategy as more is learned about product acceptance?

When Will Your Business Become Financially Viable?

What is your new product or service worth to those who will be purchasing it? Should you price the product or service based on costs or based on its value to the customer? Build a financial model with which you can determine when your new business will become profitable, including expense and investment to continue to grow the business. This will serve as a guide as to how much capital you will need to raise and invest in your business. Your investors will require this information.

Understand the Cost of Failure

Can the new initiative be undertaken in such a way that failure won't sink the company? The higher the risk, the greater the importance of understanding the cost of failure and how failure can be mitigated.

Seek the Opinions of Others

It is a strength, not a weakness, to ask the opinion of others, even if one has complete authority to make a decision on an initiative. Many times, through discussion, an alternative path on how to proceed emerges, better than the one originally contemplated.

Do Your Employees Have the Skills to Make Your Business a Success?

Are the employees you hire the right people? If it turns out that they are not the right people, part company with them. The longer they stick around and are not replaced with other, more competent individuals, the more time and capital you will waste. *The right people and capital are the most important assets of any start-up or business initiative.*

Walk Away from a Failed Initiative Sooner Rather Than Later

It may be difficult for an entrepreneur to walk away from their idea if it appears it will not be successful. When to walk away is a matter of personal judgment. Should you push ahead trying to make an idea successful or cut your losses and move on to something new?

Learn from Past Experience

Every significant initiative should be reviewed after an appropriate period of time so that learnings can be applied to future initiatives. When I became the CEO of PQ Corporation, the board asked that my team and I review all acquisitions from the past two decades to determine what went right, what went wrong, and what we would do differently when making acquisitions in the future. This was an arduous and lengthy process, but very valuable. In the five years I was CEO, we made seven acquisitions, all accretive, which helped drive our strategic and financial performance.

Learn and apply the lessons from your past successes and failures. It will lower the risk of your future initiatives.

Albert Einstein once said, "If you have never failed, you have never tried anything new." Winston Churchill said, "Success is not final, failure is not fatal. It is the courage to continue that counts." Both quotes describe the traits of all successful people, especially entrepreneurs.

Failure happens. It is not the end of the world. Learn to mitigate risks. Fred DeVito, author of Barre Fitness, once wrote, "If it doesn't challenge you, it doesn't change you." Get outside of your comfort zone. You never know where the future will take you.

CHAPTER 3-12

Be an Effective Negotiator

Figure 3-12 When negotiating, the objective is to find more overall value for both sides.

Photo: Coompia77 Collection/Getty Images

Throughout your career you will be negotiating with others. Many of these will be everyday interactions of give-and-take with low stakes. Other interactions will be more formal with much higher stakes.

I've spent years negotiating many types of deals and observing the negotiating styles and skills of other senior leaders. With that perspective, I thought I would share what I have learned about being an effective negotiator.

Know What You Are Trying to Accomplish

What would success look like? If you don't know where you want to go, you will never get there. What are the minimum outcomes you must achieve? If you cannot achieve them, are you prepared to walk away from the table? If not, perhaps you have not yet properly defined your minimum outcomes.

Develop a Game Plan Before Negotiations Start

Do you need this deal more than the other party, or do they need it more than you? Are you dealing from strength, or are you in a weaker position? Are the concessions you need to make not in your short- or long-term best interests?

Every negotiation requires compromise and trade-offs. You are not going to win on every issue. Therefore, it is important to determine the issues that are deal-breakers for you. Try to determine which issues are deal-breakers for the other side, and decide if you can live with them.

Study and Understand Your Counterpart

Understand the negotiating style of the lead negotiator on the other side of the table. What is their reputation and track record in past negotiations with you and with others? Can they be trusted to meet their negotiating table commitments?

Listen to the other party and ask questions to further understand what they want to accomplish. Communicate to them what you want to accomplish. Identify where your goals overlap and where they don't so you can work to close the gaps.

Work Toward a Win–Win

If you have an ongoing relationship, it's important for a win–win result. If one party feels they were treated unfairly in a negotiation, the relationship between the parties could be damaged and may affect future negotiations. Maintaining a good relationship in the long run is more important than a win–lose result.

A negotiation style that damages a business and personal relationship should be avoided. *The key is to attack issues, not people.* In sports, you want to defuse, not enrage your opponent in what you say before a game. In a business negotiation, it's the same: You don't want to enrage your counterpart on the other side of the table. When the tables are turned and they have the advantage in a future negotiation, they might act like you have acted, to your detriment.

If this is a one-off negotiation, you need to decide how hard you want to take advantage of your perceived strengths and drive toward a "win–lose result." You could run into the other party again in a different situation where you may not have as strong a position. People have long memories.

One of the objectives of a negotiation, through the process of give-and-take, is to find more overall value for both sides, perhaps not apparent before negotiations start.

Avoid Negotiating with Yourself

Once you make an offer, wait until the other side responds with a counteroffer. If you put another offer on the table before a counteroffer is made, the other side will view this as a weakness and try to exploit it to their advantage.

To avoid not receiving a counteroffer, ensure that your offer is credible. If it isn't, the other side may just ignore it, prematurely ending negotiations.

React Strongly to an Untrustworthy Party at the Negotiating Table

I once was the lead negotiator for my company in a negotiation to sell our ownership in a joint venture to our partner. After the second time the attorney for our partner misrepresented what we had negotiated in the agreement he was drafting, my team and I abruptly stood up and announced we were leaving the table and would not return until my counterpart replaced that attorney.

Two days later, my counterpart apologized and informed me he was appointing a new attorney to record our decisions, and negotiations resumed.

Don't misrepresent what was previously negotiated. It damages your credibility.

Remember that It Takes Two Parties to Negotiate or Renegotiate a Deal

If either party feels it is not in their best interest to do a deal, they won't. Even if you perceive you are in a position of strength and you feel you can force the other side to acquiesce to your terms, they always have other alternatives, which, if pursued, might hurt you in the long run.

Before entering a negotiation, be well prepared. Know when you are willing to walk away. Understand your situation and that of the other party, including strengths, weaknesses, and alternatives. If you are in a long-term relationship with the other party, drive for a win–win. Exercise caution driving for a win–lose. People have long memories, and you might encounter them again, perhaps when they are in a position of relative strength.

CHAPTER 3-13

You Are Now Unemployed. What Should You Do?

It could happen to anyone during their career—you lose your job. Your employer could part company with you for any number of reasons. You need to move forward and search for another job. The following guidance, developed over years of personal experience and coaching others, will help you in this process.

Never Burn Bridges

If you depart your employer on good terms, they may be willing to help you obtain future employment by being a reference or introducing you to potential employers in their network.

Remain on friendly speaking terms with your former boss and the HR department. By not burning bridges, they may be more willing to help you land your next job through their industry connections and provide a recommendation for you.

The Process of Landing Your Next Job Starts with Your Reputation at All Your Former Jobs

A future employer will perform due diligence on you. To the extent possible, they will ask your former bosses and colleagues with whom you have worked about your character, ethics and integrity, your accomplishments, and your strengths and weaknesses.

What type of leader are you? It's one thing to hold your direct reports to high expectations. It's another if you are a tyrant, micromanage your direct reports, or permit a tyrant who works for you to damage the organization below them.

If you feel that you have a legal case against a former employer, think twice about filing a suit, which becomes public information. You need to consider the pros and cons of doing so and weigh how it may affect future employment opportunities. You are much better off negotiating a settlement, which by its nature never becomes public.

Differentiate Yourself from Your Peers in Every Job You Hold

Just as businesses differentiate themselves to gain competitive advantage, individuals need to do the same. You will need to differentiate yourself from all of the other individuals applying for a job. In your resume, differentiate yourself so you are one of the few candidates invited in for an interview.

During the interview, talk about innovations that you have developed and initiated. Describe the results you have achieved that have helped your previous employers advance their business. Give examples of how you are tenacious, customer/client focused, and embrace continuous improvement.

Talk about how you have de-risked your decisions, and how effective you have been at selling your ideas. Describe how you are team-oriented and how you have empowered your direct reports by encouraging them to develop a feeling of personal ownership in what they do.

Get Out of Your Comfort Zone to Build Additional Skills

At each job that you hold, take advantage of opportunities to advance your skills and build experience that will qualify you for future assignments. Volunteer for projects outside of your comfort zone.

Manage Your Personal Brand

- Ensure your bio, resume, and LinkedIn profile are always up to date.

- Write and publish articles in areas of your expertise and of interest to readers on industry trends. Speak at industry events.
- Build a Twitter following and become known as a thought leader and influencer in your industry. Be careful not to reveal confidential business information in what you say or write.
- Develop a reputation as being a top performer by potential employers, so that they come after you when a job opens within their organization.

Network, Network, Network

Most likely, you will get your next job through people you know who are aware of a job opening within their company or within the company of a colleague. Meet with those who you know and ask them for job search advice and guidance. Ask them to introduce you to others who might also give you advice and guidance.

When You Are the Boss ...

When it comes time to part company with one of your direct reports, treat that individual with dignity and respect. That's how you would like to be treated.

The day you start a new job, you are preparing for the search for your next job by building your resume. You will look back and realize that going through the job search process, albeit challenging, was an opportunity to grow as an individual and as a professional.

Interviewing for a CEO Position? Be Prepared to Respond to These Five Questions

As a former CEO and as a current director and trustee on a number of boards, periodically I am asked to interview candidates for senior leadership positions at for-profit and nonprofit organizations. By the time I am asked to interview a candidate, they have gone through the vetting process regarding their skills, experience, and results they have achieved during their careers. Therefore, I focus on five questions about an individual's value system and leadership style, which based on my experience indicates a lot about whether the candidate will be effective and successful.

If you are the interviewer of a candidate for a senior leadership position, ask these questions. If you are the candidate being interviewed, decide how you would respond to them.

- What does tone at the top mean to you, and what tone will you set for your organization?
- What is the corporate or institutional culture you will nurture within your area of responsibility?
- When hiring direct reports, what attributes do you look for, and how will you search for and select the very best people to work for you?
- How would you describe your leadership style?
- How will you lead, motivate, and inspire every employee within your organization to achieve great results?

Tone at the Top

Effective leaders set the tone at the top, which are the organization's values and ethical standards. I want to know what tone at the top means to the candidate.

As CEO of PQ Corporation, a firm operating in 19 countries with 56 plant locations, I was concerned with how our 2,000 employees around the world would conduct business. This went beyond following company operating standards, policies, and procedures and obeying the laws of the countries in which we operated. I wanted to make sure that all employees conducted business in an ethical manner. This tone is established by the CEO, the executives reporting to the CEO, and continues on down through the organization.

Employees want to work for ethical companies, and customers want to do business with these kinds of companies. Boards of directors want to know that the senior leadership team will embrace the right values and do the right thing.

Corporate and Institutional Culture

What type of culture will the candidate nurture? Culture includes how employees interact and treat each other. When an individual makes a mistake, my expectation is that they will own it, and not shift the blame to others. This destroys trust and working relationships. Once you lose an individual's trust, it is very difficult to gain it back.

Senior leaders are always sending signals not only to their direct reports, but to all those within their organization. Some leaders send signals that they want to maximize the results of their own respective organizations, but that might result in not maximizing the results of the company as a whole. Within this organizational culture, there is little to no synergy among units. Many times, it is harder to deal with and get things accomplished within the company than with customers in the marketplace.

Hiring Direct Reports

One of the most important responsibilities of any leader is to hire the right direct reports with strong interpersonal skills. The success of any organization depends on it. I want to learn how candidates approach hiring their direct reports, and whether they look for people stronger than they are. This is a sign of self-confidence. I want to know if they hire "yes people" or individuals who will share how they really feel.

An ineffective leader at any level of the organization causes damage to the mission of that organization and to their direct reports. I once worked for a tyrant, and nearly left the company until I learned how to deal with him. Had I left, the company would have been deprived of its future CEO who significantly moved the company forward. That's how important it is to hire the right direct reports and remove those who do not measure up. It is poor leadership to continue to have a tyrant report to you.

Leadership Style

I ask each candidate to describe their leadership style. Most interviewees are sufficiently skilled and experienced to know how to answer this question, so I ask them to share examples of how they have put their leadership style into practice. Candidates that empower their people, encourage them to develop a sense of ownership in what they do, and hold them accountable for achieving results are the types of leaders you want to hire.

As a former CEO, I expected complete transparency from my direct reports. As a board member, I expect complete transparency from CEOs. Transparent leaders engender trust.

Inspiring Employees

If a leader can't inspire the employees of their organization to achieve great results, they are not the right person for the job. Leaders need to communicate the mission of the organization, what role each employee plays in executing the mission, nurture a sense of ownership in the employee for their role, and create the environment that will help them be successful.

You may ask if I have always practiced the leadership principles described in this book. The answer is no. I have learned them throughout my career. Learning how to be an effective leader is a journey, one that never ends. I am still on that journey, as are most effective leaders.

Your First 100 Days as the New CEO

You were just appointed CEO at a new company. The press announcements have been singing your praises, outlining your previous positions, expertise, and track record of results.

The employees at your new company are wondering about your leadership style, your tone at the top, and what changes you might make to the company's culture and strategy, as well as possible changes to the senior leadership team reporting to you. Your board of directors will be wondering the same thing. What you say and do will be watched intently by everyone within the organization. Expectations that you will move the company forward will be very high.

As the new CEO, what should you focus on during your first 100 days? The knowledge gained during this learning process will help you formulate changes to the culture, the senior leadership team, as well as both the operational and strategic initiatives of the company.

Listen, Ask Questions, and Form Impressions

Get to know the individuals reporting to you, as well as those individuals reporting to them Communicate to your direct reports the expectations you have of them. Assess whether they are the right people for the job.

Learn About the Norms and Practices Established by the Former CEO

- Understand the tone at the top and organizational culture under your predecessor.

- Did the culture permit employees to practice common sense and good critical judgment, and when necessary violate the rules when doing so was in the best interest of the company?
- Were employees who did so terminated or celebrated?
- How much leeway were employees given to do what's right versus following existing policies and procedures?

What Is the State of the Company's Strategic Plan?

Talk to your staff to understand the company's current market situation. Is the strategic plan current, and are the various areas within the company pursuing strategies to achieve this plan?

Has a SWOT analysis (strengths, weaknesses, opportunities, and threats) been performed recently? Do the strategic and operational plans build on the company's strengths, address weaknesses, exploit its opportunities, and defend against its threats?

When you are sufficiently knowledgeable about the business, you will need to discuss with the board the changes you want to make to the company's strategic plan. It is crucial that as CEO, you and your team "own" the strategic plan, because you and they will be held responsible for executing it.

What Is the Competitive Position of the Company?

Vis-a-vis the competition, what is the competitive position of the company's various businesses? How active is the competition in attacking the company's markets with new product offerings or aggressive product pricing?

Determine if members of the senior leadership team know why their customers buy from the company, and why other customers buy from the competition. This knowledge should be known throughout the organization, so every employee, even those who do not directly interact with the customer, can perform their jobs in a way to strengthen the company's competitive advantage and deliver a great customer experience.

What is the cost position of the company versus its competitors? How competitive is the company's business processes and information technology systems?

Ensure all employees are committed to the process of continuous improvement. The company should be on a journey to be the best in the world at what it does. Learn if all employees and board members buy into and share ownership of this ethos.

What Is the Company's Financial Position?

- How strong is the profitability and cash flow of the company and how much debt is on the company's balance sheet?
- How capital intensive is the company and what major capital projects are on the horizon?
- Is the cash flow and balance sheet sufficiently strong to fund these projects?

Ensure you are comfortable with the signature authority of your direct reports, beyond which they need to get your approval.

Learn About the Senior Leadership of the Company

Understand the leadership style, tone, and culture of the senior leaders reporting to you.

- Do they listen to their direct reports and do they surround themselves with people who will point out the brutal facts of reality?
- Can they execute and deliver results? Do they inspire their employees?
- Do they micromanage their direct reports, or do they empower them to make decisions, so they have a feeling of ownership in what they do?
- Are employees allowed to take risks, and do they know how to de-risk their decisions?
- Do some of your direct reports need to be changed?

Develop a Good Relationship with Your Board and Stakeholders

- Understand how the board operates, and their expectations of you.
- What level of information detail do they require to oversee the company?
- How much experience does each have as a board member?
- Do they tend to drift beyond oversight and governance and get into operational issues, which is the purview of the CEO?

You should also spend time focused externally, speaking with major stockholders and customers, and understand their expectations. What would they like to see that's different from the previous CEO?

In my conversations with current and former CEOs, they all commented that trust among the leadership team is paramount to the success of their organizations. The foundation of trust is honesty, ethics, and integrity. What is the level of trust among members of your senior leadership team?

Focusing on the areas above will ensure that you have an effective start as CEO at your new company.

Get Out of Your Comfort Zone, Take Risks, Fly High, and Never Compromise Your Ethics or Integrity

Figure 3-16 Stan Silverman delivering commencement speech to graduates of Drexel University, School of Medicine. Courtesy, Drexel Univeristy

As the former chairman of the board of Drexel University's College of Medicine and as the current vice chairman of the board of Drexel, I have the honor each year of addressing the University's College of Medicine graduates. I always try to share some advice that may help them navigate their careers.

At the commencement on May 17, 2019, I shared the following message:

Graduates, you have just completed an enormous undertaking. As you seek solutions to the challenges you will face, I urge you to remember what you learned here about the power of teamwork, and the importance of interpersonal skills in accomplishing your goals.

Many of you will dedicate your lives to the practice of medicine, healing the sick. Others will become researchers, or work in other areas of the healthcare profession. You will be making a difference in the lives of others, working toward the betterment of the human condition.

The best advice I can share with you as you pursue your careers is to be open to new opportunities that come your way and embrace change—the only constant in life. In addition to taking advantage of opportunities that come your way, I encourage you to be proactive and create your own opportunities. You never know where these might take you.

I am a chemical engineering graduate from your university, who just happens to be the vice chairman of its board. How does that happen? How does an engineer become the vice chairman of the board of his alma mater?

Shortly after becoming CEO of my company, I was honored to be asked to join the Drexel board of trustees. The following year, I was named chairman of the board's finance committee. A number of years later I became chairman of Drexel's College of Medicine, followed by being named vice chairman of the university's board.

I can look back to the first day after my commencement and recall the steps along my career pathway. I took advantage of opportunities and accepted assignments outside of my comfort zone to learn and to broaden my knowledge and experience. I took risks. Sometimes I failed, but I never let that stop me from moving forward.

Failure happens. It is not the end of the world. Learn to mitigate risks. Winston Churchill once said, "Success is not final, failure is not fatal. It is the courage to continue that counts." Get outside of your comfort zone. You never know where the future may take you.

Many of you will choose to advance the state of the art of your profession in areas that make a positive difference in people's lives. Many of you will work to change the world and make it a better place. There is no higher calling.

Take advantage of opportunities to do something new and different. And someday, you may have the honor of addressing graduates at their commencement ceremony, as I am doing today.

The story of Icarus, a character in Greek mythology, is a great metaphor for how one should manage their career. According to legend, Icarus flew too high, too close to the sun. The wax holding the wings to his back melted and he crashed into the sea.

Should Icarus have played it safe and flown lower, avoiding the risk presented by the sun?

Seth Godin, the author of The Icarus Deception: How High Will You Fly?, writes, "It is far more dangerous to fly too low than too high, because [you think] it feels safe to fly low. [However], we settle for low expectations and small dreams and guarantee ourselves less than what we are capable of. By flying too low, we shortchange not only ourselves, but also those who depend on us, or might benefit from our work."

During your career, be sure you don't fly too low. Take risks and fly high, and if you crash, you will pick yourself up and fly again.

The following personal attributes will help you advance in your career:

- Your commitment to yourself and others to always strive for excellence
- How you differentiate yourself by doing new things, and proactively implement positive change in everything you do
- Your interpersonal skills and how you lead others
- Your common sense and good critical judgment
- Your contacts and personal network
- Your ethics, your integrity, and your professional and personal reputation among your colleagues, your patients, and the public

During your career, be sure to protect your good name, integrity, and reputation. Once damaged, it is very difficult to earn them back.

There's a passage in the West Point Cadet Prayer that reads "Make us to choose the harder right instead of the easier wrong..."[28] Remember this, especially when you run into situations that require difficult ethical decisions.

Good luck, and may the wind always be at your back.

---

[28] https://westpoint.edu/about/chaplain/cadet-prayer

We Can Learn from Leaders Who Are Excellent Role Models and from Those Who Are Not

CHAPTER 4-1

Leadership, Teamwork, and Athletics

Watching a grandchild grow each year as an athlete and as a leader is a gift. My now 15-year-old grandson Andrew has played baseball, basketball, and soccer since the age of 4, and excels in all three sports. Watching him grow as one of the leaders of his team brings a special pride.

When Andrew was 10 years old, his basketball team was behind by 14 points at the half. He took a leadership role and told his discouraged teammates that on a prior team on which he had played, they were down by 12 points at the half, but won by 2. Andrew rallied his team and told them they could win this game. The team came back and won the game by six points.

I have watched time and time again as Andrew drives the soccer ball down the field, swarmed by his opponents. Rather than take a low probability shot on goal, he passes off to a teammate who scores. Andrew knows it is more important for his team to get the goal than for him to score. He gets credit for the assist. His teammate—the other forward—does the same when he has the ball. This is teamwork at its finest—watching two well-coached 10-year-olds who have the maturity and presence of mind to do what some adults never learn—you can accomplish more as a team than you can as an individual.

To get perspectives on how athletics builds leaders and teamwork, I interviewed Eric Zillmer, the athletics director at Drexel University; Denise Dillon, Drexel's head coach of the women's basketball team; and Alicia Aemisegger, a former student athlete who swam for Princeton University. Aemisegger is a 12-time Ivy League champion, Princeton's top female student athlete of 2010, and an Olympics trial finalist. She now works for Morgan Stanley in their real estate investment group.

I asked Zillmer how an athlete's experience on the playing field mirrors what they will experience later in life. He said,

> In athletics, you are put into a real situation, a millisecond to millisecond intense reality where you have to make decisions and work closely with your teammates to win the game. This is great training for what a student athlete will face in their careers. Athletics builds mental toughness and focus. Athletics teaches how to bounce back from adversity. You are not going to win every game, and in life, you are not going to be successful every time.

So, are leaders born or bred? Zillmer, Dillon, and Aemisegger all agree it's both. However, sometimes it takes a critical situation to bring leadership out in an individual. Dillon tells the story of how in March 2012 Drexel lost a basketball game to the University of Delaware by three points. She, her coaches, and her players were very disappointed. A senior on the team, Holly Mershon, told her fellow teammates to come out of the funk and to stop thinking about the loss and to focus forward.

In April 2013, Drexel won the Women's National Invitational Tournament championship, the first national championship won by a university women's team in Philadelphia. Dillon said regarding Mershon, "You never know when you will be called to step up and take the mantle of leadership."

Aemisegger shared with me what she learned about leadership as a student athlete. She said, "On swim teams, leaders emerge. The best leader is not necessarily the best swimmer on the team. Everyone has a chance to be a leader at different times and in different situations."

Aemisegger said she learned important lessons that carried over to her career: "Focus on the task at hand—winning, motivating teammates, sacrificing your own glory for the sake of the team and its accomplishments, building a strong work ethic, and relating to people. Athletics gives you real-life experience working with a team."

I asked Zillmer, Dillon, and Aemisegger to name their top three favorite sports movies. All three named *Miracle* as one of the three. *Miracle* is the story of the 1980 U.S. hockey team that won the Olympic gold medal. I asked them their favorite scene from that movie, and it was unanimous—it was not the scene when the U.S. team beats the Russians—it was the scene where coach Herb Brooks has the team skating sprints after a lackluster tie playing the Norwegian national team prior to the Olympics. This is also one of my favorite sports movies, and my favorite scene.

After many sprints, the team is completely exhausted and just prior to the next sprint, player Mike Eruzione unexpectedly calls out his name and his home town. When Brooks asks, "Who do you play for," Eruzione responds, "I play for the United States of America." Prior to this, the response by team members had always been the name of the college they played for—the wrong answer. After Eruzione's response, Brooks says, "That's all gentlemen," and the sprint session ends. *A great lesson—as an athlete, you play as a team, not as an individual. As a member of your company, you do the same.*

To quote Brooks during the sprints, "When you pull on that jersey, … the name on the front is a hell of a lot more important than the one on the back." I think we can all learn from Brooks and all the athletes who teach us about leadership and teamwork.

CHAPTER 4-2

Lessons from a Record-Setting NCAA Basketball Game

Figure 4-2 Sports provides a great metaphor for life. Never quit, never give up.

Photo: Josh Blake/Getty Images

What does a college basketball coach say to his players at halftime when his team is down by a significant margin? How does he inspire his team to come back and win the game?

As a business leader, when faced with adversity, what is the source of your inspiration, and how do you inspire your team?

An NCAA record was set on February 22, 2018,[29] when Drexel University's men's basketball team, down by 34 points at the end of the first

[29] https://ncaa.com/news/basketball-men/article/2018-02-23/9-numbers-drexel-basketballs-rally-biggest-comeback-ncaa

half by a score of 53-19, defeated University of Delaware 85-83. It was the largest comeback in NCAA Division 1 history.

I interviewed Drexel coach Zach Spiker to get his perspective on the game and to learn what he said to his team in the locker room at halftime.

Inspiring a Turnaround

I asked Spiker, "In a game like the one against Delaware, or any game in which your opponent has a significant lead, what goes through your mind? How do you inspire your players to turn the game around?"

Spiker responded:

As we do in every game, the coaching staff met for a few minutes at the start of halftime to formulate our message. We talked about what was going well and what needed improvement. For this game, we wanted to boost our team's belief that they could play a strong second half by improving offensive and defensive execution and by playing with a higher energy level.

It certainly wasn't a normal halftime locker room, but we didn't need to "peel the paint off the walls," which could hurt the team's confidence. We needed to build their confidence so that they could get back into the game.

Delaware played a near-perfect first half and at the same time, we didn't play well. We told the team, "Let's play our best in the second half and see what happens."

Sticking with the System

A sign of discipline of any team is the ability to stick with the system they have learned, practiced, and played for months, even when behind, rather than change the game plan to something new. The team, however, could certainly improve its execution.

Spiker referred to a February 19, 2018 ESPN[30] article in which legendary Villanova University basketball coach Jay Wright described a game

---

[30] http://espn.com/mens-college-basketball/story/_/id/22436614/inside-villanova-epic-five-year-run

against North Carolina State University. Villanova was trailing NC State. Wright said, "… [during the game], two seniors … kept saying, 'Keep playing Villanova basketball, just keep doing what we do.'"

Wright continued: "They went out dying on their own sword, like Samurai warriors. If you're going to go out, you're going to go out our way. They're legends for how they handled adversity."

Spiker and his coaching staff inspired their team, saying:

Let's play Drexel basketball. Let's play as hard as we can for the name on the front and on the back of your jersey. Play for Drexel, play for the fans, play for your families—play for everything and everyone you represent. Let's play for what Drexel is, and what we want Drexel to become.

Spiker said:

We told the team not to look at the scoreboard and not to worry about what occurred in the first half. The score now starts at 0-0. Let's see how we do in each of the four-minute media segments during the second half.

Slowly but surely, the gap in the score narrowed until Drexel achieved its two-point victory.

Never Give Up

All business leaders have been in similar situations where they needed to inspire their team to win in a tough competitive environment.

"This is what all races are about. This is what life is about."[31]

These are the inspirational words flashed across the screen at the end of a YouTube video (courtesy of love2246) that teaches that one should never quit, never give up. Runner Heather Dorniden of University of Minnesota fell during the March 2008 Big Ten 600-meter final with

---

[31] https://youtube.com/watch?v=NsOBaV_93yQ

200 meters to go. Rather than quit the race, she got up, caught the other runners, and won the race in a close photo finish.

Drexel's second half comeback victory in their basketball game against Delaware and Dorniden's photo finish after falling during her race are inspirational lessons for all of us. Sports provides a great metaphor for life. Never quit, never give up. This is what life is about.

We Should All Possess the Leadership Traits of Colonel Joshua Chamberlain

As leaders, how do we win the hearts, minds, and confidence of the people within our organizations so that they are fully invested in the organization's mission?

There is much to be learned from the traits of effective military leaders. One such leader is Colonel Lawrence Joshua Chamberlain.

Chamberlain was a 34-year-old commander of the 20th Maine Volunteer Infantry Regiment of the Union Army during the Civil War. He was previously a language professor at Bowdoin College, and one of many ordinary people who volunteered to serve their country.

Chamberlain was a modest, determined, and understated leader with fierce resolve and intense will, qualities identified in successful leaders by Jim Collins in his book, *Good to Great*. Chamberlain's honesty, integrity, ethics, and sense of honor made him a very effective leader.

In his classic novel *Killer Angels*, historian Michael Shaara wrote a historical account of the Battle of Gettysburg extracted from the journals of those who fought in the battle.

Great Leaders Possess Emotional Intelligence

Shaara writes of an incident in which Chamberlain is given custody of 120 Union mutineer prisoners just prior to the battle of Little Round Top. He was granted authority to shoot any prisoner who refused to follow his orders. Rather than threaten these soldiers, he took a different approach. He needed them to strengthen his regiment for the upcoming battle. A prisoner tells Chamberlain, "They been tryin' to break us by not feedin' us," so Chamberlain gives them food and water.

Private Bucklin from the group approaches Chamberlain and says that he was selected to tell him of the prisoners' grievances. Chamberlain listens intently rather than ignore him.

In a reenactment of Chamberlain's speech to the prisoners[32] from the film *Gettysburg* (YouTube video courtesy of Bill Toth), he says,

> I've been talking with Private Bucklin. He's told me about your problems. There's nothing I can do today. We'll be moving out in a few minutes. We'll be moving all day.
>
> I've been ordered to take you men with me. I've been told that if you don't come, I can shoot you. Well, you know I won't do that. Maybe someone else will, but I won't.
>
> The whole reb army is up the road a ways waiting for us … We can surely use you fellows. We're well below half-strength and whether you fight or not, that's up to you.
>
> You know who we are and what we're doing here. … This regiment was formed last summer, in Maine. There were a thousand of us then. There's less than 300 of us now. … [We came for different reasons.] Many of us came because it was the right thing to do.
>
> This is a different kind of army. If you look at history you'll see [that] men fight for pay … or some other kind of loot. … But we're here for something new. … We're an army out to set other men free …
>
> If you choose to join us, if you want your muskets back nothing more will be said. If you won't join us, you'll come along under guard. When this is over I'll do what I can to see that you get fair treatment. … Gentlemen, I think if we lose this fight, we lose the war. So, if you choose to join us, I'll be personally very grateful.

The way in which Chamberlain treated and spoke to these men had the intended effect. He demonstrated his respect for them and gave them a purpose. All but 6 of the 120 mutineers chose to join him, significantly

---

[32] https://youtube.com/watch?v=uTZSwgnWtuA

increasing the strength of his regiment, possibly making the difference in the July 2, 1863 pivotal defense of Little Round Top.

Holding their position at Little Round Top against attacks by the Confederate Alabama 15th Regiment was an imperative. Chamberlain was told by his commanding officer, "You cannot withdraw under any conditions. If you go, the line is flanked, and they'll go right up the hilltop and … [attack us from the rear]. You must defend this place to the last." A Union loss at Little Round Top could have changed the outcome of the Battle of Gettysburg, the Civil War, and perhaps the course of history.

Chamberlain's regiment held the high ground, which gave it an advantage over the Confederates, but they had suffered heavy losses and were running out of ammunition. They risked being overrun.

Effective Leaders Inspire Their Followers. They Lead from the Front

In an inspiring, spine-tingling reenactment[33] (YouTube video courtesy of Zandalis) of the battle from the film *Gettysburg*, Chamberlain says "We can't run away… We can't shoot. So, let's fix bayonets." Chamberlain decides to take the initiative and go on the offensive.

Chamberlain tells his men,

We'll have the advantage of moving downhill. [Captain] Ellis [Spear], you take the left wing. I'll take the right. I want a right wheel forward of the whole regiment … We charge … swinging down the hill. Understand? Does everyone understand?

His officers respond in unison, "Yes sir."

Chamberlain screams the bone-chilling commands "BAYONETS" and "CHARGE!" With their swords held high, Chamberlain and Ellis lead their courageous men into a fierce bayonet attack down the hill. The Confederates fire at near point-blank range at the charging regiment, but not being mentally prepared to face bayonets, are overwhelmed and either

---

[33] https://youtube.com/watch?v=ZL-5uyp44WA&t=10s

killed, retreat, or surrender. Through a valiant effort, Chamberlain and his regiment hold Little Round Top.

After the Civil War, Chamberlain was awarded the Medal of Honor for his defense of Little Round Top. Chamberlain's bayonet charge was pivotal in the Union's victory at Gettysburg and the Civil War.

Why was Chamberlain's leadership during the defense of Little Round Top so effective? He was a visible leader who led from the front. He communicated to his men the importance of the mission and their role in fulfilling it. His men respected and trusted him because Chamberlain respected and trusted them. They gave Chamberlain their loyalty and maximum effort. We as business leaders will never face the life and death situations that our military leaders do, but we can all learn from the inspirational leadership of Joshua Chamberlain.

Amtrak's Joe Boardman— Out in Front When Tragedy Hits

The derailment of Amtrak Train 188 in Philadelphia on May 12, 2015 was a major tragedy, resulting in 8 fatalities and over 200 injuries. The cause of the derailment was the train traveling at 106 mph, more than double the speed limit for the section of track, going into a curve.

Amtrak's CEO, on the Scene

I was struck by the way Amtrak CEO Joe Boardman was out front and center, the public face of Amtrak. In a letter to the public, Boardman wrote, [34]

> With truly heavy hearts, we mourn those who died. Their loss leaves holes in the lives of their families and communities. On behalf of the entire Amtrak family, I offer our sincere sympathies and prayers for them and their loved ones. Amtrak takes full responsibility and deeply apologizes for our role in this tragic event.

Boardman went beyond this statement. He was on the scene in Philadelphia and made himself available for interviews by the news media. He was one of the speakers at a memorial service held on May 18, attended by the first responders and government officials, at the site of the derailment.

---

[34] https://time.com/3881606/amtrak-derailment-letter/

In a moving speech, Boardman expressed his regret and extended his condolences to the families of those whose lives were lost. Based on the tone and the emotional way in which he made his remarks, everyone knew he meant it.

Effective Leaders Aren't Evasive

In an interview with CNN,[35] Boardman was asked, "[When you] heard the news [that the train was traveling at] 106 miles per hour in a 50 mile per hour zone, what was your initial feeling?" Boardman stated, "We knew … that was too fast." He was asked, "What do you say to people who say if [Positive Train Control] was installed, it could have prevented this fatal accident?" Boardman responded, "Had it been installed, it would have prevented this accident."

Some CEOs choose to remain in the shadows, relying on their public relations people to handle an event of this magnitude. Boardman demonstrated courage for choosing to be out in front. This is a responsibility that cannot be delegated. Boardman showed he cared by being open and transparent. People will question for a long time why Amtrak had not yet installed Positive Train Control on this section of track. What they won't question is Boardman's decision to be the public face of Amtrak.

What lessons can the leaders of all organizations learn from Boardman? When a tragedy occurs due to your company's action or inaction, its reputation will be damaged. You can help it recover by being the public and human face of your company. Take responsibility, show genuine sympathy for the victims, and vow to take steps to ensure that a similar incident doesn't happen again.

---

[35] https://video.search.yahoo.com/search/video?fr=yfp-t&p=cnn+boardman+int erview+amtrak+crash#id=1&vid=337739ed200e3f71fee2aba20e9d3817&actio n=click

Saxbys: Servant Leadership Pays Dividends

Figure 4-5 Interior of a Saxbys coffee shop, Philadelphia. Courtesy, Saxbys.

CEOs are always looking for ways to differentiate their business from other providers to create a competitive advantage. One of the ways to achieve this differentiation is through a servant leadership environment and a continuous improvement culture.

Leaders of High-Performing Companies Are People Centric

In an April 28, 2013 article in *The Washington Post* headlined "Servant leadership, a path to high performance,"[36] Edward D. Hess at the University of Virginia wrote,

> Leaders [of high performing companies] are servants in the best sense of the word. They are people-centric, value service to others and believe they have a duty of stewardship. Nearly all are humble and passionate operators who are deeply involved in the details of the business. ... They have not forgotten what it was like to be a line employee.
>
> They believe that every employee should be treated with respect and have the opportunity to do meaningful work. They lead by example, live the "Golden Rule," and understand that good intentions are not enough—behaviors count. These leaders serve the organization and its multiple stakeholders. They are servant leaders.

What Hess found is very similar to the research of Jim Collins as presented in his book *Good to Great,* in which Collins describes "Level 5 leaders [as those who] display a powerful mixture of personal humility and indomitable will." Level 5 leaders are not the "larger than life" imperial leaders many of us are so familiar with.

Don't think that servant leaders and Level 5 leaders hold their organizations accountable to only easily achievable goals. They set tough goals and have high-performance expectations for their employees, empower them to achieve those expectations, and hold them accountable for results.

Nick Bayer of Saxbys

Founder and CEO of Saxbys, Nick Bayer is one such leader. Bayer is an ardent believer in servant leadership. He feels that Saxbys' culture is the most important determinant of his company's success.

---

[36] https://washingtonpost.com/business/capitalbusiness/servant-leadership-a-path-to-high-performance/2013/04/26/435e58b2-a7b8-11e2-8302-3c7e0ea97057_story.html?utm_term=.b85d88212de6

I asked Bayer, "How do you differentiate Saxbys? Why do customers come to your cafés and buy coffee?" He said,

We compete on people, not on product. Most people think that we are in the product business. We are actually in the people business. I realized that I can compete [with other companies] on people and on hospitality. People, our team members and our guests, are at the core of what we do.

Bayer and his senior leadership team give significant support to their café managers. He said,

I personally am an absolute zealot of the mentality of "servant leadership." Organizations work best when they are upside down. Our café managers are the CEOs (café executive officers) of their businesses. All the people at headquarters exist to serve our café managers and their teams. We are here to help them to be successful at their jobs. My expectation of them is to be servant leaders to the members of their teams. Their job is to make life better for their guests every single day.

Repeating Bayer's statement: *"All the people at headquarters exist to serve our café managers and their teams. We are here to help them to be successful at their jobs."* This is how leaders of corporate staff units should see their responsibilities: *to help the line managers be successful.* The line managers in companies are the ones who generate revenue and earnings by providing a great customer/client experience. Staff units don't generate revenue or earnings. They are there to support the line units.

On the subject of empowerment, Bayer said,

We hire people with good critical judgment and empower them to make decisions. Other employers take power away from their employees. I don't want to get in the way. I want my people making decisions. I hire people who will develop a sense of ownership in their business.

Giving Students Management Responsibility

In 2015, Saxbys opened a café on the campus of Drexel University, a café entirely managed by Drexel undergraduate students. It has a different feel than its chain-based competitors. The atmosphere is "millennial trendy," including the background music. Saxbys team members engage in friendly conversation with customers, who are referred to within the Saxbys culture as guests.

I asked Bayer why he decided to pursue the idea of having a Saxbys café managed and operated by college students. He said, "I saw college students who were looking for entrepreneurial opportunities, I saw colleges embracing entrepreneurship, and I felt that I wanted to provide the experiential component."

Bayer continued,

> I thought that if you take people who are smart, passionate and prideful, and give them the tools and wide enough boundaries, good things could happen. I want this to be a place where people want to work. Our culture is defined by our people, not by a product.

The first manager of Drexel's Saxbys café was Meghan Regan, at the time a pre-junior on a six-month co-op work assignment. After being trained as a manager at other Saxbys locations, she assumed her role as manager of the first Saxbys café on Drexel's campus while it was being constructed. She was responsible for marketing the café and hiring the staff—all Drexel students.

Regan told me, "I think the culture is amazing. Every Saxbys I worked at [during my training] felt like home. People come first. Team members are friendly with their guests and get to know their names." Regan said,

> If guests need to wait to be served, we apologize and give them a free drink card or ask if we can get them a cookie to enjoy while they wait. We ask them how their day is going … we don't want them to be bored while waiting in line.

So, what are the takeaways on how to build your business and differentiate it from the competition, regardless of the business that you are in? Hire people with strong interpersonal skills and with good critical judgment, empower them, and create a culture where the focus is on creating a great customer experience. Treat employees, guests, customers, and clients like you would like to be treated. Lead your employees like you would like to be led. The businesses that adopt these principles are the ones that will excel.

Leadership Lessons from
The Imitation Game

The Imitation Game received eight Oscar nominations in 2014, including best picture. The film is about Englishman Alan Turing (brilliantly played by best actor nominee Benedict Cumberbatch) and his small team of elite mathematicians and code breakers who broke the "unbreakable" German Enigma code during World War II. This permitted the British to successfully use a captured German Enigma machine to decode military messages that turned the tide of the war.

Film critics gave *The Imitation Game* and its actors high marks in many categories. After reading dozens of reviews of the film, I could not find one that mentioned three of the themes that ran through the film: a lesson in counterintuitive leadership, breaking paradigms, and the importance of respecting the abilities of women.

Don't Discount a Counterintuitive Leadership Style

Turing lacked interpersonal skills and would have failed as a leader in most situations. As a team member, he alienated his fellow code breakers. He was driven, however, by his strong belief that "... only a machine could defeat another machine."

Prior attempts at breaking the Enigma code by humans using traditional methods were unsuccessful. In spite of having no interpersonal skills, he slowly wins his team over with an unwavering resolve that his approach was the only one that would break the code. His team develops ownership in Turing's approach, and threatens to quit when the naval commanding officer who heads the Enigma project wants to fire Turing.

The military had no faith in anything outside of their own narrow inflexible framework for breaking the code.

Break Paradigms to Achieve Breakthrough Results

The only way to break the Enigma code was to break traditional paradigms and approach the code-breaking task in a completely different way—building an electromechanical machine, one of the first computers. The commander who heads the Enigma project was someone who could only think in traditional terms. He says to Turing, "Have you ever won a war? ... It's done through order, discipline [and] chain of command. ... You will do as your commanding officer instructs." *Talk about not empowering direct reports and not cutting them loose to do their thing!*

Turing then asks the naval commander who his commanding officer is, and he responds, "Winston Churchill." Turing sends a letter to Churchill, complaining about the oppressive environment that was slowing his work. As a result of that letter, Churchill puts him in charge of the code-breaking project. Had Turing acquiesced and played by the rules of "order, discipline [and] chain of command," the Enigma code would not have been broken, and World War Two could have lasted many more years.

Bureaucracy Hinders Creativity and Innovation

Turing's passionate belief that his approach was right drove him to jump the chain of command. He broke through a bureaucracy that was crushing innovation and creativity. Many initiatives that require a rapid pace and out-of-the-box thinking are often pursued outside of the formal organization and away from bureaucracy.

Recognize and Respect the Abilities of Women

After Churchill put Turing in charge of the code-breaking project, he searches for additional candidates for his team. Code-breaking candidates prequalified by completing a newspaper crossword puzzle in less than 10 minutes. When a prequalified woman, Joan Clarke (played by supporting actress Oscar nominee Keira Knightley) is late for the next round of problem-solving qualification, she is barred from entry.

It is assumed that Clarke could only be in the building to apply for a secretarial position and is directed to where secretarial candidates are screened. As a woman, Clarke is not viewed as someone who would have prequalified as a code breaker. When she protests that she in fact did prequalify for this next round of qualification, she is not taken seriously until Turing intervenes and allows her to enter the room, full of only men.

The candidates are given 6 minutes to solve a problem, and Clarke is the first to solve it in 5 minutes and 34 seconds, a feat that even amazed Turing. She and only one other candidate are selected to join Turing's code-breaking team. Clarke would go on to play a key role in the project.

I am not suggesting that you practice Turing's leadership style. It worked in this unique set of circumstances that ultimately led to his and his team's success. The British military needed Turing more than Turing needed the British military. He was one of the most highly regarded mathematicians and code breakers in Great Britain, and his preeminent status protected him.

The most impactful statement in the film is, "*Sometimes it is the people no one imagines anything of, who do the things no one can imagine.*" As leaders, we need to remember that innovation and creativity comes from those who break paradigms, think differently, and take risks. Sometimes the most innovative and creative people are those who are the most unconventional. As leaders, we also need to be mindful not to let bureaucracy kill new initiatives.

One wonders how much more advanced civilization and our quality of life would be today if over the course of history, women were as respected as men and had the same opportunities based on their abilities.

CHAPTER 4-7

Turing Pharmaceuticals: Avoid Behavior That Will Come Back to Haunt You

On rare occasions, corporate leaders lose sight of a major principle in business and in life. When they take an action that in the eyes of the public, customers, or government officials is unreasonable or egregious, or act in a way that is disrespectful or with disdain, their behavior will come back to haunt them and their company.

Martin Shkreli Gives a Bad Name to the Position of CEO

Such is the case of Martin Shkreli, the former CEO of Turing Pharmaceuticals (no relation to Alan Turing in Chapter 4-6). This company acquired the rights to Daraprim, a drug used to treat toxoplasmosis, a disease that weakens the immune system of people who have cancer or are HIV positive. Turing increased the price of Daraprim from $13.50 to $750 per pill, pushing this drug out of the financial reach of many patients.

Unrelated to the Daraprim price increase, Shkreli resigned from his position as CEO of Turing Pharma after being indicted on December 17, 2015, for a crime committed prior to him joining Turing. Quoting Brooklyn U.S. Attorney Robert Capers,[37] "Shkreli essentially ran … a Ponzi scheme where he used each subsequent company to pay off defrauded investors of the prior company." Shkreli is currently serving a seven-year sentence for securities fraud.

---

[37] http://fortune.com/2015/12/17/martin-shkreli-ponzi-scheme/

Shkreli was summoned to a U.S. House Committee hearing on February 4, 2016, to respond to questions about the Daraprim price increase. During the hearing, Shkreli continually invoked his Fifth Amendment right, refusing to answer any questions which might incriminate him. Shkreli had a dismissive attitude during much of the hearing.

USA Today quoted U.S. Rep. Elijah Cummings (D-MD), as commenting[38] "Drug company executives are lining their pockets at the expense of some of the most vulnerable families in our nation. ... It's not funny, Mr. Shkreli. People are dying and they are getting sicker and sicker."

After his appearance before the House Committee, Shkreli tweeted[39] it's "hard to accept that these imbeciles represent the people in our government." His lawyer, Benjamin Brafman, chalked up Shkreli's behavior to his young age of 32 and being nervous.

This Guy Was the CEO, the Leader, and the Public Face of a Company?

Why would a board appoint an individual with these behavioral traits as CEO? Turing is a privately held company, and only two other individuals were listed as board members on the Turing website: chairman of the board Ron Tilles and Walter C. Blum. Tilles assumed the additional position of CEO on an interim basis when Shkreli stepped down from that position.

I am sure that Tilles and Blum were not happy with Shkreli's performance in front of the House Committee. *Shkreli tarnishes the public image of all business leaders. He is an embarrassment to the position of CEO.*

It is understood that the price of pharmaceuticals must not only cover a new drug's research and development, animal and human trials, and safety testing costs, but also the costs for drugs that never make it to

---

[38] https://usatoday.com/story/money/2016/02/04/martin-shkreli-congressional-testimony-turing-pharmaceuticals-valeant-fda-drug-prices/79808004/
[39] https://thehill.com/policy/healthcare/268204-shrekli-blasts-lawmakers-as-imbeciles-after-hearing

market. Without the ability to recover the cost of drug development, many lifesaving drugs would never be introduced.

Daraprim, however, is not a new drug. Turing acquired Daraprim from another company, so its research and development costs many decades ago have long since passed. Increasing the cost of Daraprim 5,500 percent shows a lack of sensitivity to patients who rely on the drug and damages the reputation of the company and pharmaceutical industry in the eyes of the public. Where was Shkreli's good critical judgment, an attribute all CEOs must have?

At the December 2015 Forbes Healthcare Summit,[40] Shkreli stated,

I probably would have raised [the price of Daraprim] higher. [It's] probably what I should have done. I could have raised it higher and made more profits for our shareholders, which is my primary duty. No one wants to say it, no one's proud of it, but this is a capitalist society, capitalist system and capitalist rules, and my investors expect to me to maximize profits, not to minimize them, or go half, or go 70 percent, but to go to 100 percent of the profit curve that we're all taught in MBA class.

Wow! Is that what was really taught in Shkreli's MBA class? He should have been taught that personal and company reputations matter, that markets and government law makers react.

Industries and the companies within those industries are given a license to operate by the public. The public controls this license through the lawmakers they elect, who in turn appoint regulators whose goal it is to ensure that companies obey the law and operate in a way that is not detrimental to the public interest.

Due to the rapid increase in the price of insulin over the past five years, on May 22, 2019, Colorado became the first state to put a cap on the price of insulin, making it more affordable to people that need this drug. The out-of-pocket cost is capped at $100 per month, compared with a precap cost that was more than five times higher. Capping drug

---

[40] http://nydailynews.com/life-style/health/pharma-ceo-jacked-pill-price-article-1.2455809

prices could occur with increasing frequency to ensure people can acquire the lifesaving medication they need.

President Donald Trump has called for public disclosure of the cost of pharmaceuticals in television ads, similar to how a drug's side effects must be disclosed during an ad. The pharma industry has raised concerns over confusing the public, based on a variety of insurance plans people might have which result in different drug prices. These companies need to get out in front of the tide of public opinion which is turning against them. If they don't control their own narrative and destiny, someone else will, perhaps in a way not to their liking.

Similarly, in cases where the customer is a company and it feels that it is being taken advantage of by its supplier, that company might go to the ends of the earth to find an alternate source of supply. That, Mr. Shkreli, is how the capitalist system works.

Leaders need to understand that their decisions and actions have consequences, including damage to their personal reputations and that of their company. If they act in an egregious manner, there will be a reaction that they won't like. Our reputation is the most important thing any of us have. Once lost, we never really gain our reputation back. We must carefully protect it.

Mylan N.V. There Are Consequences to Acting Like a Monopolist

Mylan N.V. CEO Heather Bresch joined the unenviable club of pharmaceutical executives who have attracted the wrath of the public, media, and members of Congress, all of whom are concerned about the affordability of lifesaving drugs.

In 2009, Mylan started to increase the price of its auto-injector EpiPen, a device that an individual can use to self-inject an emergency dose of epinephrine in the event of an allergic reaction to various foods or insect bites. The price of a package of two EpiPen auto-injectors rose to $609, a 550 percent increase over a 10-year period.

Why do pharmaceutical companies raise the prices of their lifesaving drugs beyond the point that consumers can afford? Because they can, especially if effective marketing makes it the preferred drug by physicians who prescribe it, even if a generic version exists. Consumers are exposed to the cost of a drug to the extent of their prescription insurance co-pays and deductibles.

Bresch Defends the EpiPen Price Increases

In an April 26, 2016 *New York Times interview*[41], Bresch stated, "I am running a business. I am a for-profit business. I am not hiding from that." Her statement could not have been more arrogant and insensitive to individuals who someday will need to use an EpiPen to immediately counter

---

[41] https://nytimes.com/2016/08/27/business/painted-as-a-villain-mylans-chief-says-shes-no-such-thing.html

a life-threatening allergic reaction. She sounds like Martin Shkreli, former CEO of Turing Pharma in his defense of the rapid price increase of Daraprim discussed in Chapter 4-7.

Americans Subsidize the Availability of Pharmaceuticals in Other Countries

Other countries set limits on what pharmaceutical companies can charge for drugs, which is usually a fraction of what is charged in the United States. In effect, American consumers are subsidizing the world when it comes to drug prices.

> Pharmaceutical companies need to realize that the public, through their elected government officials, grants their industry a license to operate. Government officials can make changes to that industry's license if doing so will benefit the public, as did Colorado when it placed a price cap on insulin. Bresch is right when she states, "I am running a business." She should act that way and realize that the threat of government intervention could someday be a higher risk than she thinks it is.

CHAPTER 4-9

Flint Michigan Water Crisis: A Failure in Leadership

Figure 4-9 You always want to hire, appoint, or elect people with common sense and good critical judgment who will do the right thing.

Photo: Borzeya Collection/Getty Images

The word "crises" accurately fits the description of a man-made water quality disaster in Flint, MI.

How Not to Act as a Leader

There was a complete lack of leadership by Michigan government and regulatory leaders whose actions and inactions caused this disaster. The accountability lies with Governor Rick Snyder and his executive branch staff, as well as the leadership and staff of the Michigan Department of Environmental Quality.

These leaders continually told the citizens of Flint that the water in their homes was safe, even after people reported problems with the water's color, odor, and taste. The water, in fact, was not safe. The result was that many Flint residents suffered lead poisoning due to high lead levels in their water, including children who are most susceptible to lead exposure that can result in complicated health and developmental problems.

To reduce costs, in March 2013, Flint's mayor and its City Council made the decision to switch the long-term source of Flint water from the Detroit water system to the Karegnondi Water Authority, which would build a pipeline to transport water from Lake Huron to Flint. In April 2014, to save $5 million during the remaining two-year period until the completion of the pipeline, Flint switched from the Detroit water system to the Flint River as an interim source of city water.

The water from the Flint River has a high salt content and therefore is very corrosive, causing lead and other heavy metals to leach out of aging pipes delivering water to homes. The addition of an anticorrosion agent to high salt content water is a well-established common practice to reduce heavy metal leaching from water system pipes.

The cost of the anticorrosion agent, had it been added to the Flint River water, *would have only been $100 per day.* The failure of government and regulatory authorities not to require the addition of the anticorrosion agent was a gross failure in stewardship and responsibility, which has led to criminal charges against a number of individuals involved in the Flint water decision process.

More than half of the population of Flint is African American, and nearly half of the city's population lives below the poverty line. Were the demographics of Flint a factor in the decision to switch to untreated Flint River water, as some individuals suggested? If Michigan government and environmental officials experienced the same type of water coming from the faucets in their homes, corrective action would have been demanded and immediately implemented.

It wasn't until pediatrician Mona Hanna-Attisha found elevated levels of lead in the blood of Flint children that the Flint water problem was taken seriously. Engineering Professor Marc Edwards and his team from Virginia Polytechnic Institute and State University conducted independent water quality tests and found high lead levels in tap water in homes.

Within some homes, lead levels were found to be several orders of magnitude higher than what is considered acceptable.

There is no threshold level of lead considered to be completely safe. It is estimated that as many as 12,000 residents of Flint have elevated levels of lead in their bodies. Many of these are children, who will suffer developmental issues and a range of other health problems.

In September 2019, NBC News reported[42] on the fallout from having exposed children to water with high lead levels. Michigan State data showed there was a 56 percent increase in children needing special education services. The Flint educational system lacked the trained professionals to provide these services.

Resident Water Quality Complaints Were Ignored

In a *Washington Post* article dated January 7, 2016, headlined "The poisoning of Flint,"[43] columnist Katrina vanden Heuvel wrote,

> When complaints persisted, officials assured citizens that the water was safe to drink, repeatedly disregarding clear evidence that it wasn't. But when elevated levels of lead showed up in children's blood this past fall, the government was forced to admit[44] there was a problem.
>
> Snyder appointed a task force to investigate the crisis, which found, among other things, that legitimate fears were met with "aggressive dismissal, belittlement, and attempts to discredit"[45] the individuals speaking out.

---

[42] https://nbcnews.com/today/embedded-video/mmvo69562949764

[43] https://washingtonpost.com/opinions/the-poisoning-of-flint/2016/01/19/5462112c-be02-11e5-9443-7074c3645405_story.html?utm_term=.b20da6201d14

[44] https://nytimes.com/2015/10/08/us/reassurances-end-in-flint-after-months-of-concern.html?_r=2

[45] https://nytimes.com/2016/01/10/us/flint-wants-safe-water-and-someone-to-answer-for-its-crisis.html

In a January 16, 2016 story by NBC News[46], Snyder's then chief of staff, Dennis Muchmore, acknowledged the administration's deplorable response in a July 2015 e-mail, writing,

> I really don't think people are getting the benefit of the doubt. Now they are concerned and rightfully so about the lead level studies they are receiving. *These folks are scared and worried about the health impacts and they are basically getting blown off by us (as a state we're just not sympathizing with their plight).*

Flint water was switched back to the Detroit water system until the pipeline from Lake Huron was completed. In the interim, the National Guard distributed bottled water to Flint residents.

Snyder declared a state of emergency in Flint on January 5, 2016.[47] He has also acknowledged his role in this crisis. "Accountability" and "austerity" has been Snyder's political narrative. Was austerity partly to blame for the Flint water crisis? Due to the weak financial condition of the city, Snyder had appointed a series of emergency managers to oversee the finances of Flint, and it was one of these emergency financial managers that signed off on the switch to Flint River water.

The Flint Advisory Task Force appointed by Snyder to investigate the crisis has stated, [48]

> Throughout 2015, as the public raised concerns and as independent studies and testing were conducted and brought to the attention of … *[Michigan Department of Environmental Quality], the agency's response was often one of aggressive dismissal, belittlement, and attempts to discredit these efforts and the individuals involved.*

---

[46] https://nbcnews.com/health/health-news/internal-email-michigan-blowing-flint-over-lead-water-n491481

[47] https://washingtonpost.com/news/morning-mix/wp/2016/01/06/michigan-governor-declares-state-of-emergency-over-lead-levels-in-water-in-flint-mich/?utm_term=.21d1042c132f

[48] https://mlive.com/news/flint/2015/12/five_takeways_for_the_flint_wa.html

... We find both the tone and substance of many MDEQ public state-
ments to be completely unacceptable.

You always want to hire, appoint, or elect people with common sense
and good critical judgment who will do the right thing. The leadership
of the MDEQ did not meet this standard, and neither did the governor
of Michigan and his executive branch staff. In the future, why should
the citizens of Flint believe anything they are told by their governmental
leaders? These leaders have lost their credibility.

Tone at the top and institutional culture play a critical role in the suc-
cess of any organization. Michigan government and regulatory leaders were
horribly lacking in both. They did not fulfill their responsibility to protect the
people of their state.

Whether a government or regulatory leader, the CEO of a company, or head of a nonprofit organization, these leaders' constit-
uents—the public, employees, or stockholders—are counting on
them to do the right thing. The Flint, MI, water crisis is a lesson
in how not to act as a leader.

Wells Fargo Scandal: Failures in Leadership, Management, and Corporate Governance

The Wells Fargo scandal went public in May 2015 when the bank was sued by the district attorney of Los Angeles for fraudulent sales practices within the Community Banking Division that had taken place over the previous five-year period. It was ultimately revealed that bank branch employees opened 3.5 million unauthorized customer deposit and credit card accounts to meet unrealistic sales goals. Wells Fargo violated the trust of its customers through unethical sales practices. *If you can't trust your bank, who can you trust?*

In a press release, the Consumer Financial Protection Bureau stated, [49]

> Spurred by sales targets and compensation incentives, employees boosted sales figures by covertly opening accounts and funding them by transferring funds from consumers' authorized accounts without their knowledge or consent, often racking up fees or other charges.

Wells Fargo was fined $185 million and ordered to reimburse customers $5 million in fees they were charged as a result of these practices. The cost to the bank of lost business due to the loss of customer's trust was much higher.

---

[49] https://corporatecrimereporter.com/news/200/cfpb-fines-wells-fargo-100-million/

Prior to her retirement in July 2016, Carrie Tolstedt was the senior vice president of Consumer Banking at Wells Fargo where the abuses occurred. During her last five years in that position, her compensation continually rose. It was not apparent that her performance reviews and compensation were adversely impacted by her unit's continued unethical sales practices. Instead, she reaped the benefits of these dishonest acts.

Why Did the Wells Fargo Board Wait So Long to Hold Stumpf Accountable?

As a former CEO, I would have reported the unethical sales practices to my board as soon as they were known to me. The board's expectation would be that I would fix the issue. Would my board have tolerated this issue continuing for five years? No! I would have been fired for not fixing the issue, and for continuing to treat our customers in an unethical manner and putting the reputation of the company at risk. So, where was the Wells Fargo board for these five years?

When Tolstedt's retirement was announced, Wells Fargo CEO John Stumpf praised her[50] as "one of the most valuable Wells Fargo leaders, a standard-bearer of our culture, a champion for our customers, and a role model for responsible, principled and inclusive leadership."

This is a strongly supportive statement about a leader whose unit within the bank violated the trust of its customers. Didn't Stumpf realize that his statement lacked credibility in the eyes of the bank's retail branch employees who felt pressure every day to act unethically?

On April 10, 2017, the directors of the Wells Fargo board independent oversight committee issued their 111-page report[51] on the scandal that had engulfed the bank. The report was prepared by the law firm Shearman & Sterling LLP. Reading the Shearman & Sterling report, the following lessons stand out.

---

[50] https://wallstreetinsightsandindictments.com/2016/09/the-situation-at-wells-fargo-is-worse-than-we-thought/

[51] https://www08.wellsfargomedia.com/assets/pdf/about/investor-relations/presentations/2017/board-report.pdf

Don't Lose Sight of Your Company's Mission

The mission of every business should be to exceed its customers' expectations and provide them a great customer experience. It was apparent that this was not the mission of the Community Banking Division of Wells Fargo.

The Community Banking Division only cared about increasing sales revenues, which drove incentive compensation. This was a significant failure of the culture of the bank. The report stated, "The Community Bank identified itself as a sales organization, like department or retail stores, rather than a service-oriented financial institution. This provided justification for a relentless focus on sales, abbreviated training and high employee turnover."

I found it strange that Wells Fargo referred to its bank branches as stores. Wells Fargo's branches are not stores. They are banks providing clients with banking services. Why did Wells Fargo cheapen its brand?

An Incentive System Not Properly Designed Can Produce Adverse Results

Quoting from the Shearman & Sterling report:

> The root cause of sales practice failures was the distortion of the Community Bank's sales culture and performance management system, which when combined with aggressive sales management, created pressure on employees to sell unwanted or unneeded products to customers and, in some cases, to open unauthorized accounts.

This sales pressure was intense. A *Wall Street Journal* article by Emily Glazer on September 16, 2016, was headlined "How Wells Fargo's high-pressure sales culture spiraled out of control."[52] The article was

---

[52] https://wsj.com/articles/how-wells-fargos-high-pressure-sales-culture-spiraled-out-of-control-1474053044

subheadlined "Hourly targets, fear of being fired and bonuses kept employees selling even when the bank began cracking down on abuses."

Glazer's article describes a deeply embedded culture in which *lower level managers told their employees to ignore orders from senior Wells Fargo managers to stop abusive sales practices.* Many Wells Fargo employees at retail bank branches chose to quit rather than do their jobs in an unethical manner.

While Business Operations Can Be Decentralized, Internal Controls Must Be Centralized

Stumpf believed that internal control and compliance functions should be decentralized. He continued to have this belief year after year even as serious issues persisted within Consumer Banking.

Quoting the report,

Wells Fargo's decentralized corporate structure gave too much autonomy to the Community Bank's senior leadership, who were unwilling to change the sales model or even recognize it as the root cause of the problem. Community Bank leadership resisted and impeded outside scrutiny or oversight and, when forced to report, minimized the scale and nature of the problem.

One wonders why the Wells Fargo board did not identify decentralized internal control and compliance functions as a significant enterprise risk, especially as they became aware of the issues within Community Banking. These are mission-critical to any bank.

A Business Unit Leader That Is Not Transparent Should Raise Red Flags

The independent oversight committee report stated that Tolstedt

was notoriously resistant to outside intervention and oversight. Tolstedt and certain of her inner circle were insular and defensive and did not like to be challenged or hear negative information.

Senior leaders within the Community Bank were frequently afraid or discouraged from airing contrary views.

Tolstedt effectively challenged and resisted scrutiny both from within and outside the Community Bank. She and her group risk officer not only failed to escalate issues outside the Community Bank, but also worked to impede such escalation, including by keeping from the Board information regarding the number of employees terminated for sales practice violations.

Tolstedt's toxic tone at the top of her organization was a red flag that was ignored. This type of leader can never be trusted. Stumpf should have fired her.

Employees Who Use the Employee Hotline to Report Wrongdoing Must Be Protected

In a September 21, 2016 *CNN Money* article headlined "I called the Wells Fargo ethics line and was fired,"[53] reporter Matt Egan writes that the news organization spoke with a number of Wells Fargo employees who were fired for reporting unethical practices on the ethics hotline and to the bank's human resources department.

Stumpf was forced to step down as CEO on October 12, 2016. He was replaced as CEO by Tim Sloan, who was previously chief operating officer of the bank.

In a March 18, 2017 interview,[54] Sloan was asked by CNN anchor Poppy Harlow: "Almost half a dozen Wells Fargo workers told *CNN Money* that they were fired after they called the bank's confidential ethics hotline. … What was your personal reaction when you heard some of this?"

Sloan responded,

[53] https://money.cnn.com/2016/09/21/investing/wells-fargo-fired-workers-retaliation-fake-accounts/index.html

[54] https://money.cnn.com/2017/04/19/investing/wells-fargo-ethics-line-ceo-tim-sloan/index.html

One instance of retaliation from my perspective is one too many. It's completely unacceptable … I think about employees that had a concern, that were uncomfortable going to their manager or didn't bring it up to our Human Resources group and instead called the ethics line. If they were retaliated doing that, that's completely unacceptable to me.

Perhaps these employees didn't trust HR. What did the audit committee of the board do after they learned of the ethics hotline reports? Ignore them?

On March 28, 2019, Tim Sloan announced that he was stepping down from his role of chairman and CEO of Wells Fargo. He was chief operating officer of the bank during the years the Wells Fargo scandal occurred and was tainted by it. I was surprised he was appointed CEO after Stumpf left the bank.

What can CEOs and board members learn about the Wells Fargo scandal? *Ensure your company's value statement is more than just words on paper, don't tolerate senior executives who are not transparent, and don't ignore a toxic culture.* It only gets worse and becomes harder to change. Be aware that some employees may sacrifice ethical standards to generate large bonuses. Put in place controls to ensure this does not occur. The reputation of your company and the trust of your customers depend upon it.

Hopefully, what went wrong at Wells Fargo will be a lesson for other companies with respect to the proper tone at the top, corporate culture, and corporate governance.

CHAPTER 4-11

Volkswagen Employees Responsible for "Dieselgate." Where Was Your Legal, Ethical, and Moral Compass?

Figure 4-11 Volkswagen, where was your legal, ethical, and moral compass?

Photo: Vesilvio Collection/Getty Images

The CEO or a division executive is incentivized to deliver stellar financial and growth results with a demanding and intimidating style that causes some subordinates to violate ethical norms or the law. Does the CEO or division executive think they won't get caught? What does this say about the individual, the senior leadership team, the board, and the culture of the organization?

Did Volkswagen Think They Would Not Get Caught?

In the years prior to 2015, Volkswagen deliberately installed software on diesel cars that would give lower than actual readings during the emissions testing process. Not only did this action permit these cars to pass emission tests, the results were also used in Volkswagen's strategy to market their "clean diesel" vehicle technology. *Volkswagen, where was your legal, ethical, and moral compass?*

When questioned about diesel car emissions, Volkswagen at first denied there was an issue. Management knew full well that they were gaming the testing protocols. It was only after the EPA threatened to withhold certification of the company's new car model did Volkswagen come clean and admit to the fraud.

After the Dieselgate scandal became public in October 2015, the company's stock price tumbled. Volkswagen CEO Martin Winterkorn was forced to resign and has been charged with defrauding customers and investors. James Liang, the Volkswagen engineer who wrote the software to give false emission readings, has been sentenced to 40 months in prison. Oliver Schmidt, one of Volkswagen's compliance officers, received a prison sentence of seven years.

The global cost to Volkswagen is estimated to be $136 billion[55] to date. That is what can happen when a company acts unethically and violates the law.

Culture Dictates Behavior

In a January 2016 article in *Entrepreneur Magazine*, "The biggest lesson from Volkswagen: Culture dictates behavior,"[56] Robert Glazer wrote, "Culture is a powerful force that can cause people to make decisions that aren't in their companies' best interests."

---

[55] https://statista.com/statistics/665397/costs-resulting-from-volkswagen-diesel-emission-scandal/

[56] https://entrepreneur.com/article/254178

Glazer said,

CEO Martin Winterkorn was a demanding boss who abhorred failure. Former executives described his management style as authoritarian and aimed at fostering a climate of fear. A culture that discourages open dialogue and limits checks and balances can prompt cheating and fraud. A culture with high standards that accepts failures as growth opportunities, on the other hand, benefits both the company and employees.

So, whose job is it to watch for the tell-tale signs that the CEO is so demanding that subordinates act unethically or violate the law to achieve results in order to please the CEO? It is the board's job. For the direct reports of the CEO, it is the CEO's job to ensure his or her senior team does not act in an unethical or illegal manner.

Boards Are Important in Monitoring Tone at the Top and Organizational Culture

How is unethical or illegal activity uncovered? By the audit committee of the board and how it responds to reports that come through the employee hotline. By ensuring that there is a system of controls and checks and balances surrounding the accuracy of key metrics. If data for these metrics are not checked and verified, there could be serious adverse consequences to the company if they are incorrect due to fraudulent intent.

Sabine Vollmer wrote in the July 2018 issue of the *Journal of Accountancy*,[57] "Boards that prioritize corporate culture, watch for red flags and set clear expectations will encourage ethical behavior throughout the company." Vollmer said, "Research over the past 20 years has continued to underscore that integrity drives performance. *Corporate culture and tone at the top are considered key drivers of ethical behavior, but boards of directors often devote little time to the topic.*"

---

[57] https://journalofaccountancy.com/issues/2018/jul/corporate-board-role-ethical-culture.html

Having once worked for a boss whose style was similar to that of Volkswagen's Winterkorn, being promoted around him, eventually becoming his boss, and then firing him, I have first-hand knowledge of the damage this type of boss can cause. I replaced that fired individual with the best general manager within the company at the time, who changed the culture of that organization.

Shortly after the start of my tenure as the president of one of my company's worldwide businesses, I called a meeting of all our country managers to launch our continuous improvement program and to develop our operating principles. On that list was "We would obey the laws of the lands in which we operate," an important principle that sometimes needs to be expressed explicitly.

Rex Tillerson, former chairman and CEO of Exxon Mobil and former secretary of state under President Donald Trump, in his departure comments from the U.S. State Department said, *"Never lose sight of your most valuable asset, the most valuable asset that you possess: your personal integrity."*[58]

Tillerson continued, "Only you can relinquish [your integrity] or allow it to be compromised. Once you've done so, it is very, very hard to regain it. So guard it as the most precious thing you possess." Did the leaders at Volkswagen not think of this?

My message to boards and to CEOs:

Don't tolerate individuals that act unethically or violate the law. Fire them, even if they are meeting or exceeding their financial and growth objectives. They are not worth keeping around. When their unethical or illegal activity becomes public, it will cause significant reputational and monetary damage to your organization.

A major responsibility of the board is to hire and fire the CEO. The board is also responsible for ensuring compliance to the laws of the countries in which the company operates, as well as assessing tone at the top and corporate culture. These are the areas that can seriously hurt the company's reputation in the eyes of government regulators, investors, and customers.

---

[58] https://cnsnews.com/news/article/melanie-arter/tillerson-farewell-speech-can-be-very-mean-spirited-town

Lessons from the Theranos Debacle

What is the responsibility of a CEO to their investors? For public companies, there is a legal responsibility to follow the Securities and Exchange Commission (SEC) rules and regulations pertaining to disclosing material events and providing accurate information about the financial and operational condition of the company.

For private companies, the obligation to disclose is not as well prescribed. However, the CEO still has a responsibility to disclose pertinent information to the company's shareholders and prospective investors, so they can make informed investment decisions about the company.

The Obligation of a CEO Is To Be Honest and Ethical

It shouldn't be necessary, but one would hope this is taught in business school. Privately held start-up Theranos, founded in 2003, is a case in point. On June 15, 2018, the Department of Justice announced[59] that a federal grand jury indicted Theranos CEO Elizabeth Holmes, a Stanford University drop-out, and former president Ramesh Balwani, charging them with wire fraud and conspiracy to commit wire fraud associated with false claims about the performance of the portable blood analyzer manufactured and marketed by the company.

The indictment follows charges by the SEC on March 14, 2018, against Theranos, Holmes, and Balwani for deceiving the company's investors. Quoting the SEC press release,[60]

---

[59] https://justice.gov/usao-ndca/pr/theranos-founder-and-former-chief-operating-officer-charged-alleged-wire-fraud-schemes
[60] https://sec.gov/news/press-release/2018-41

> Numerous false and misleading statements [were made] in investor presentations, product demonstrations, and media articles by which they deceived investors into believing that its key product—a portable blood analyzer—could conduct comprehensive blood tests from finger drops of blood, revolutionizing the blood testing industry.

Steven Peikin, co-director of the SEC's Enforcement Division, commented,

> Investors are entitled to nothing less than complete truth and candor from companies and their executives.[61] The charges against Theranos, Holmes, and Balwani make clear that there is no exemption from the anti-fraud provisions of the federal securities laws simply because a company is non-public, development-stage, or the subject of exuberant media attention.

Many tests purported to have been performed on a Theranos-developed blood testing device were actually tested by the company on other commercially available testing devices. Holmes and Balwani also claimed their products were deployed by the U.S. Department of Defense in Afghanistan, but it was discovered this never happened. They further claimed revenue for their company would reach over $100 million in 2014 but ended up only generating $100,000.

Due to hyped-up claims that were not accurate, Theranos attracted over $700 million from investors. At its peak, the company was valued at $9 billion.

Sure, investing in start-ups is risky, and investors should understand those risks. However, investors have an expectation that the CEO will not make false and misleading claims. *Does Holmes feel any remorse for defrauding these investors? Where was her ethical compass?*

What happened at Theranos begs the question, where was the company's board and why was there a breakdown in the governance process?

---

[61] https://sec.gov/news/press-release/2018-41

Were they blind to what was going on? Did they understand their oversight and fiduciary responsibilities to prevent false disclosures by the company?

The Company's Directors Must Be Knowledgeable in the Area of Corporate Governance

The Theranos board consisted of luminaries such as Henry A. Kissinger and George P. Shultz, both high-profile and well-respected elder statesmen who served in the administrations of former presidents in a variety of high-level positions, as well as former senators Bill Frisk and Sam Nunn. Secretary of Defense Jim Mattis once served on the board.

These individuals have excelled during their careers, but one must ask *what do they know about corporate governance or enterprise risk management? Why didn't they hold Holmes accountable for the claims the company was making?* It appears as if they were appointed to the board as window dressing to give an aura of credibility to Theranos. They should have done their job and held Holmes to high ethical standards.

Whether a privately held start-up or established public company, directors have a duty of care and a duty of loyalty to the company and its investors.[62] These directors need to have board governance expertise. Investors should be able to rely on them to do the right thing. Did the directors of Theranos know these duties? Their personal reputations depended on it, but more importantly, it is the right thing to do.

---

[62] https://resources.lawinfo.com/business-law/the-board-of-directors-duties-of-care-and-loy.html

Massey Energy Mine Disaster: Leaders Have a Responsibility to Keep Their Employees Safe

Figure 4-13 Employee safety in the workplace is the CEO's responsibility

Photo: Ostill Collection/Getty Images

The CEO has the ultimate responsibility for employee safety in the workplace. The board's role is to hold the CEO accountable not only for the safety of the company's employees, but also for the company's environmental performance. These should be included in the metrics the board uses to evaluate CEO performance.

Massey Energy: "A Failure of Basic Coal Mine Safety Practices"

In April 2016, Donald Blankenship, the former CEO of Massey Energy, was sentenced to prison for 12 months after being found guilty in December 2015 for conspiring to violate federal mine safety standards. On April 5, 2010, an explosion in the Upper Big Branch (UBB) mine of Performance Coal Company (PCC), a subsidiary of Massey Energy, resulted in the deaths of 29 miners.

In May 2011, an independent investigative report titled "Upper big branch—The April 5, 2010 explosion: A failure of basic coal mine safety practices"[63] was published. The report documented instance after instance of safety violations and showed that production of coal had a higher priority than the safety of the company's miners.

The U.S. Department of Labor's Mine Safety and Health Administration (MSHA) imposed a fine of $10.8 million on Massey Energy. An MSHA report on the explosion states, "Massey's corporate culture was the root cause of the tragedy. MSHA has issued Massey and PCC 369 citations and orders … for an unprecedented 21 flagrant violations, which carry the most serious civil penalties available under the law." MSHA Assistant Secretary Joseph A. Main stated,

Every time Massey sent miners into the UBB Mine, Massey put those miners' lives at risk. Massey management created a culture of fear and intimidation in their miners to hide their reckless practices. Today's report brings to light the tragic consequences of a corporate culture that values production over people.

Company Safety Performance Must Be Part of the CEO's Performance Assessment

Was the Massey board ever concerned about Blankenship's poor history of compliance with federal mine safety standards and a corporate culture

---

[63] http://mineaccidents.com.au/mine-accident/180/upper-big-branch

not focused on safety? The company had a history of safety issues. Why wasn't Blankenship held accountable to a higher standard of performance by his board prior to the explosion?

The CEO Needs to Take Ownership of Health, Safety, and Environmental Performance

As CEO of PQ Corporation, I presented and discussed our quarterly safety, health, and environmental performance as the first topic at every board meeting, before discussion of financial performance. If plant employees felt that an established procedure was unsafe, they raised the issue with the plant's management. Unsafe conditions were addressed to avoid potential accidents.

Hazards were promptly addressed. A sense of ownership was instilled in employees for their personal safety and that of their colleagues. Our OSHA recordable accident rate improved, and we achieved first quartile performance within the chemical industry.

> Directors, hold your CEOs accountable for more than just financial performance. Hold them accountable for their tone at the top and the culture they nurture within their organization. The world is changing, driven by a focus on reputation, and where millennials, the future leaders of your company, want to work. Companies that do the right thing will be the ones that produce the best returns for investors.

CHAPTER 4-14

To Maximize Shareholder Return, Treat Stakeholders the Right Way

In August 2019, the Business Roundtable issued an updated statement[64] on the purpose of the corporation signed by 181 CEOs of major corporations, broadening the primary objective of maximizing shareholder return to include running a company for the benefit of all stakeholders in addition to shareholders—its customers, employees, suppliers, and communities. The CEOs committed to:

- Delivering value to our customers.
- Investing in our employees.
- Dealing fairly and ethically with our suppliers.
- Supporting the communities in which we work.
- Generating long-term value for shareholders, who provide the capital that allows companies to invest, grow and innovate.

I believe the Business Roundtable's updated statement represents the best practices of companies that want to maximize shareholder return over the long-term, but not everyone agrees.

Reactions to the Updated Business Roundtable Statement

The reactions were quick and not unexpected. The Council of Institutional Investors said,[65] "The statement undercuts notions of managerial

---

[64] https://businessroundtable.org/business-roundtable-redefines-the-purpose-of-a-corporation-to-promote-an-economy-that-serves-all-americans

[65] https://www.cii.org/aug19_brt_response

accountability to shareholders." A *Wall Street Journal* editorial stated,[66] "It's ... notable that the CEOs for America's biggest companies feel the need to distance themselves from their owners." I disagree with both viewpoints.

Quoting The New York Times reaction,[67] "[The Business Roundtable's updated statement] was an explicit rebuke of the notion that the role of the corporation is to maximize profits at all costs ... "Milton Friedman, the University of Chicago economist who is the doctrine's most revered figure, famously wrote in The New York Times[68] in 1970 that "the social responsibility of business is to increase its profits." Friedman doesn't address the broader question of how a company should do this.

As the former CEO of a global corporation, corporate director and nationally syndicated columnist on leadership and corporate governance, I have always believed that maximizing shareholder return is the measure of how well a company treats its stakeholders—its customers, employees, suppliers, and communities, as well as the cost effectiveness of its operations. All boards need to hold their CEOs accountable for the safety of their employees and environmental performance. They must not treat fines from regulatory authorities as just part of the cost of doing business.

Many companies agree with this philosophy. However, there are companies that in the past have harmed some of its stakeholders in a quest to maximize shareholder return. Well-known recent examples include, Turing Pharmaceuticals (Chapter 4-7), Mylan NV (Chapter 4-8), Wells Fargo (Chapter 4-10), Volkswagen (Chapter 4-11), Theranos (Chapter 4-12), and Massey Energy (Chapter 4-13).

> As CEOs, we need to treat our customers, employees, suppliers, and communities in the right way and operate our companies in an ethical manner. This is how to maximize shareholder return over the long term. The Business Roundtable updated statement on the purpose of the corporation is consistent with this principle.

---

[66] https://www.wsj.com/articles/the-stakeholder-ceos-11566248641

[67] https://nytimes.com/2019/08/19/business/business-roundtable-ceos-corporations.html

[68] https://nytimes.com/1970/09/13/archives/article-15-no-title.html

Learn How To Be an Inspiring Leader

What makes a truly great leader? In part, it's the ability to inspire followers toward an aspirational goal. I miss the inspirational leadership of three former leaders, whose words and their delivery of those words inspired many of us.

Former President John F. Kennedy, in his September 12, 1962 speech (YouTube video courtesy of 0 Sallent)[69] announcing the goal of sending men to the moon before the decade was out and returning them safely to Earth, was an inspiration to many. As a high school student at the time with the goal of going to college and earning a degree in chemical engineering, I was inspired by not only Kennedy's audacious challenge to overcome the immensely difficult technical and engineering barriers, but also his confidence that the goal could be achieved.

Former President Ronald Reagan, in his January 20, 1981 inaugural address (YouTube video courtesy of Denise c),[70] (courtesy of Denise c) spoke of the exceptionalism of Americans in a very positive, uplifting message, describing the "will and moral courage of free men and women," and how committed we are to defending freedom. Reagan's eloquent speech was a call to action for all Americans to be the best they could be and serve as an example for the rest of the world to emulate.

Former British Prime Minister Winston Churchill, in his June 4, 1940 we shall fight on the beaches speech (YouTube video courtesy of Movieclips),[71] addressed Parliament to rally his citizens during World War Two. Churchill's speech, reenacted by Gary Oldman, in the film

---

[69] https://youtube.com/watch?v=kwFvJog2dMw
[70] https://youtube.com/watch?v=GiuFzpl28io
[71] https://youtube.com/watch?v=skrdyoabmgA

The Darkest Hour, is an inspiring example of how a national leader can mobilize a nation's citizens toward the most challenging goal it has ever faced—national survival. In the film, one can overhear the comment, "He mobilized the English language, and sent it into battle." Unfortunately, not very many of our political leaders can do the same today.

What did Kennedy, Reagan, and Churchill have in common? They had a wonderful command of vocabulary and knew how to inspirationally communicate their goals and beliefs with emotion in an uplifting way that won the hearts and minds of their citizens. They united the nations they were leading at the time.

How does a business leader win the hearts and minds of those they lead? How do you become an inspiring leader? Certainly, it takes more than great communication skills. Inspirational leaders have other skills as well.

Lolly Daskal, an executive leadership coach, wrote a blog titled "Six powerful traits of the most inspiring business leaders,"[72] in which she identifies these traits as people skills, credibility, authenticity, emotional intelligence, motivation, and positivity.

Murray Newlands, an entrepreneur, business advisor, and speaker, in his article, "Seven characteristics of inspirational leaders,"[73] says that inspirational leaders have a clear vision of the future, express unerring positivity, listen to their people, are grateful to their team, communicate impeccably, are trustworthy, and are passionate about what they do.

Based on my own experience as a CEO and director on the boards of numerous companies, I would like to add to the list of characteristics and traits of inspirational leaders identified by Daskal and Newlands, as follows:

Is Genuine in Words and Actions, and Is a Person of High Ethics and Integrity

A leader who is not genuine and lacks ethics and integrity will not earn the respect and trust of the people within their organization. They will certainly not inspire followers to achieve great results.

---

[72] https//lollydaskal.com/leadership/6-powerful-traits-of-the-most-inspiring-business-leaders/

[73] https://entrepreneur.com/article/252916

Communicates the Importance of the Company's Goals

The senior leadership team of the company needs to communicate the importance of the company's goals in both group meetings and one-on-one conversations with key opinion leaders within the company. Employees need to feel that the goals are meaningful and achievable, and will have a positive benefit for them and the organization.

Identifies the Role that Employees Play in Attaining the Goal

After completing a new strategic plan, as the recently appointed CEO of PQ Corporation, I communicated the goals of the company to our business units, and just as importantly, the role each business unit had in achieving those goals. The role of our low-growth commodity chemicals and engineered glass materials businesses was to generate cash flow, through very heavy emphasis on continuous improvement. This cash flow would be invested in our high-growth specialty chemicals, catalyst, and performance materials businesses.

After I made my presentation to the employees of our commodity chemicals business, one of the employees commented, "This is the first time I was told what our role is in the achievement of the company's strategic plan." In my former position as chief operating officer of the company, I was too close to the strategic planning process to realize that the different roles of business unit employees to achieve the company's goals had not been communicated to them. All individuals who take part in achieving the goals of the company should have personal ownership of the role that they themselves play in the achievement of those goals.

Frequently Provide Updates on Progress

By frequently sharing updates on the progress toward achieving the company's goals, an inspirational leader has the opportunity to keep the focus on what the company is trying to accomplish. It keeps the company's employees in the game.

Great inspirational leaders have great communication skills. To those that have a fear of public speaking, you can conquer that fear by facing it head on, by receiving coaching, and by taking every opportunity to speak publicly. You will never regret that you developed this skill. Someday, you, like Kennedy, Reagan, and Churchill, may be able to mobilize the English language and send it into battle.

In Closing

I'd like to close with a few points of advice for readers, and hope if you remember anything, you will remember the following:

Values

- Exhibit the right tone at the top and nurture the right organizational culture.
- Always lead your organization with the highest levels of ethics and integrity.
- Embrace the timeless philosophy of continuous improvement.

People

- Differentiate yourself from your peers in every job you hold.
- Hire people with common sense and good critical judgment who will violate policy when on rare occasion, it is in the best interests of the company to do so. Hire leaders who will permit their direct reports to do so.
- Get out of your comfort zone and push your employees out of their comfort zone.
- Value the opinions of your experts and listen to the lone wolf.
- Encourage employees to develop a sense of personal ownership in what they do. Hire leaders who will permit their direct reports to do so.
- Develop other leaders, inspire those around you, and help them move to that next level.
- Don't tolerate a tyrant nor an unethical employee working for you.

- Share your expectations with direct reports, empower them, and cut them loose to do their thing.
- Know when to ask for forgiveness rather than for permission.

Markets

- Understand your markets and get ahead of market trends.
- Work to become the preferred provider of product/services to your market.
- Differentiate your company by delivering a great customer experience.
- Understand your competition.
- Recognize that only the paranoid survive.
- Face the brutal facts of reality.

Communication

- Communicate the vision and mission of the company to your employees, and their role in achieving both.
- Build your personal brand.
- Learn how to sell your ideas.
- Own your mistakes and learn from them.
- Network, network, network!

Universal Principles

- Project a proactive attitude. Be a person who sees possibilities and abundance, and not one who only sees scarcity and limitations.
- Remember the passage in the West Point Cadet Prayer, "Make us choose the harder right than the easier wrong."

- Lead like you would like to be led and treat people like you would like to be treated.

You never know where the future will take you. I am now in my fourth career: First rising through my company to the position of CEO of a global company operating in 19 countries; second, serving as a director on the boards of numerous organizations including chairman of the board of my alma mater's college of medicine and vice chairman of the board of Drexel University; third, as a nationally syndicated columnist for American City Business Journals and its subsidiary, *Philadelphia Business Journal*; and fourth, as a published author of this book.

After graduating with a Bachelor of Science degree in chemical engineering, I had two career goals: full responsibility for the P&L statement of a business unit, and becoming the CEO of a company. I was able to achieve both goals.

I got out of my comfort zone. I took advantage of opportunities that came my way and made my own opportunities. Sometimes I failed, but I never let that stand in the way of getting up the next morning and trying again. Failure is part of the learning process. During this process, I have grown as a leader and hopefully have had positive impact on others.

Failure should not stop you from moving forward. Every time we fail, we grow. There is an inspiring video (YouTube video courtesy of Jassa Vock) titled, "*Courage of Famous Failures*,"[74] which profiles legendary individuals, including Winston Churchill, Meryl Streep, Stephen Spielberg, Steve Jobs, Ludwig van Beethoven, Walt Disney, Michael Jordan, Oprah Winfrey, and Albert Einstein, who were disappointments to their parents or teachers, or who failed early in the careers before achieving great, and in some cases, legendary success.

At some point in your career, you may face a challenge so massive that it appears to be insurmountable. Fall back on your experience, expertise, emotional intelligence, and your team. When you look down into the deep, dark abyss and overcome the challenge, it becomes your finest hour.

---

[74] https://youtube.com/watch?v=Ydeyl0vXdP0

As you lead others, remember the words of Simon Sinek, renowned author and motivational speaker, "There are leaders, and there are those who lead. Leaders hold a position of power, or authority. Those who lead inspire us." What kind of leader will you be?

About the Author

A recognized thought leader and influencer, Stan Silverman is a widely read nationally syndicated columnist on leadership in the *Philadelphia Business Journal* and 42 affiliated business publications across the United States. He is the former president and CEO of global PQ Corporation and has served on numerous public, private equity, private, and nonprofit boards.

Stan is a frequent speaker on creating competitive advantage for your business and how to advance your career by being different than your peers. He has been an invited guest lecturer at the Wharton School of the University of Pennsylvania and at the LeBow College of Business of Drexel University, where he holds the position of senior executive in residence.

Stan earned a Bachelor of Science degree in chemical engineering and an MBA degree from Drexel University. He is also an alumnus of the Advanced Management Program at the Harvard Business School.

Index

FORTHCOMING TITLE IN BUSINESS CAREER DEVELOPMENT COLLECTION

Vilma Barr, Editor

- *Introduction to Business* by Patrice Flynn

Announcing the Business Expert Press Digital Library

Concise e-books business students need for classroom and research

This book can also be purchased in an e-book collection by your library as

- a one-time purchase,
- that is owned forever,
- allows for simultaneous readers,
- has no restrictions on printing, and
- can be downloaded as PDFs from within the library community.

Our digital library collections are a great solution to beat the rising cost of textbooks. E-books can be loaded into their course management systems or onto students' e-book readers.

The **Business Expert Press** digital libraries are very affordable, with no obligation to buy in future years. For more information, please visit **www.businessexpertpress.com/librarians**. To set up a trial in the United States, please email **sales@businessexpertpress.com**.

CPSIA information can be obtained
at www.ICGtesting.com
Printed in the USA
BVHW041351171220
595870BV00038B/1111